TREAD CAREFULLY
ADULTS

MAZE ULTIMATE

ActivityCrusades

Published by Speedy Publishing Canada Limited

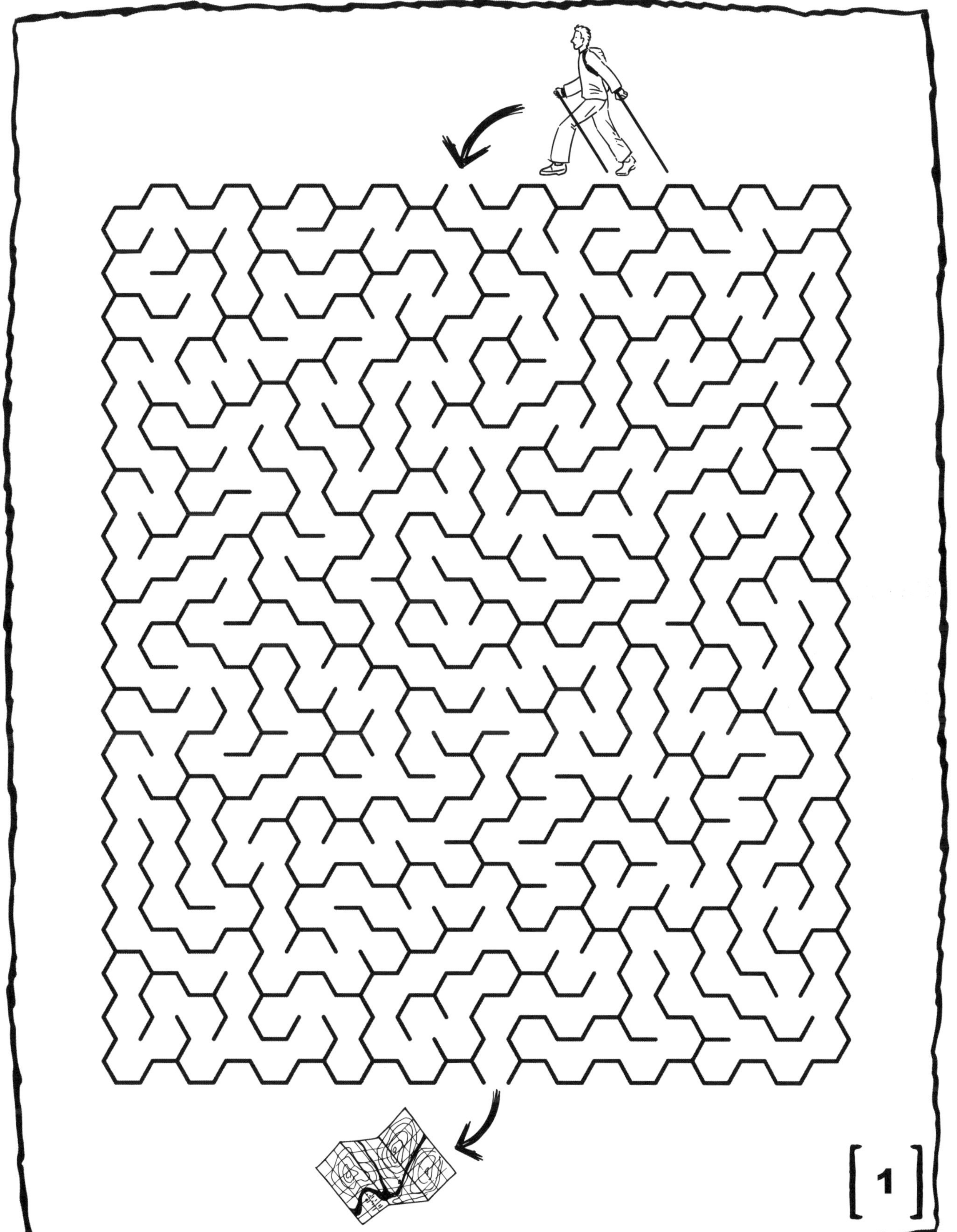

[1]

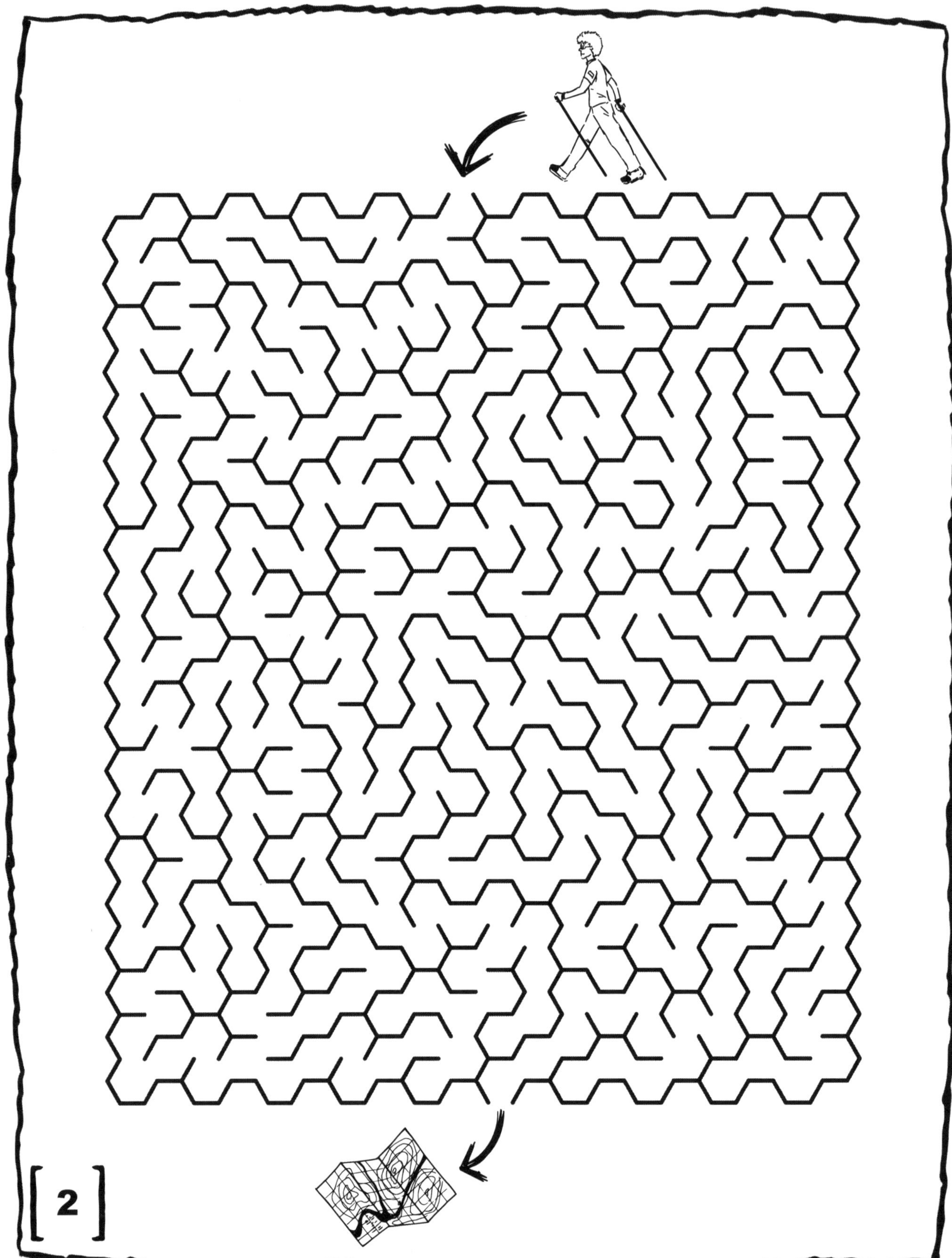

[2]

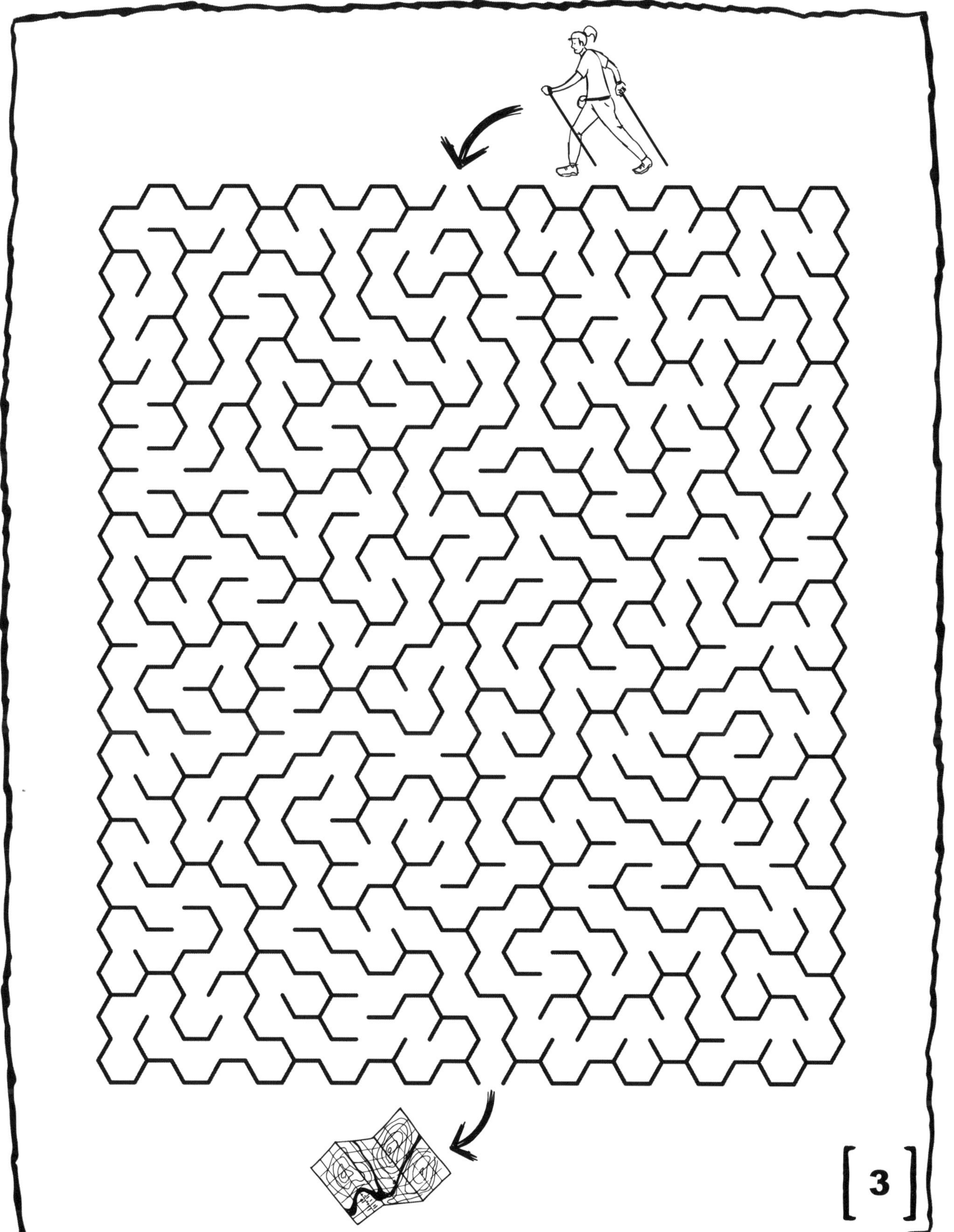

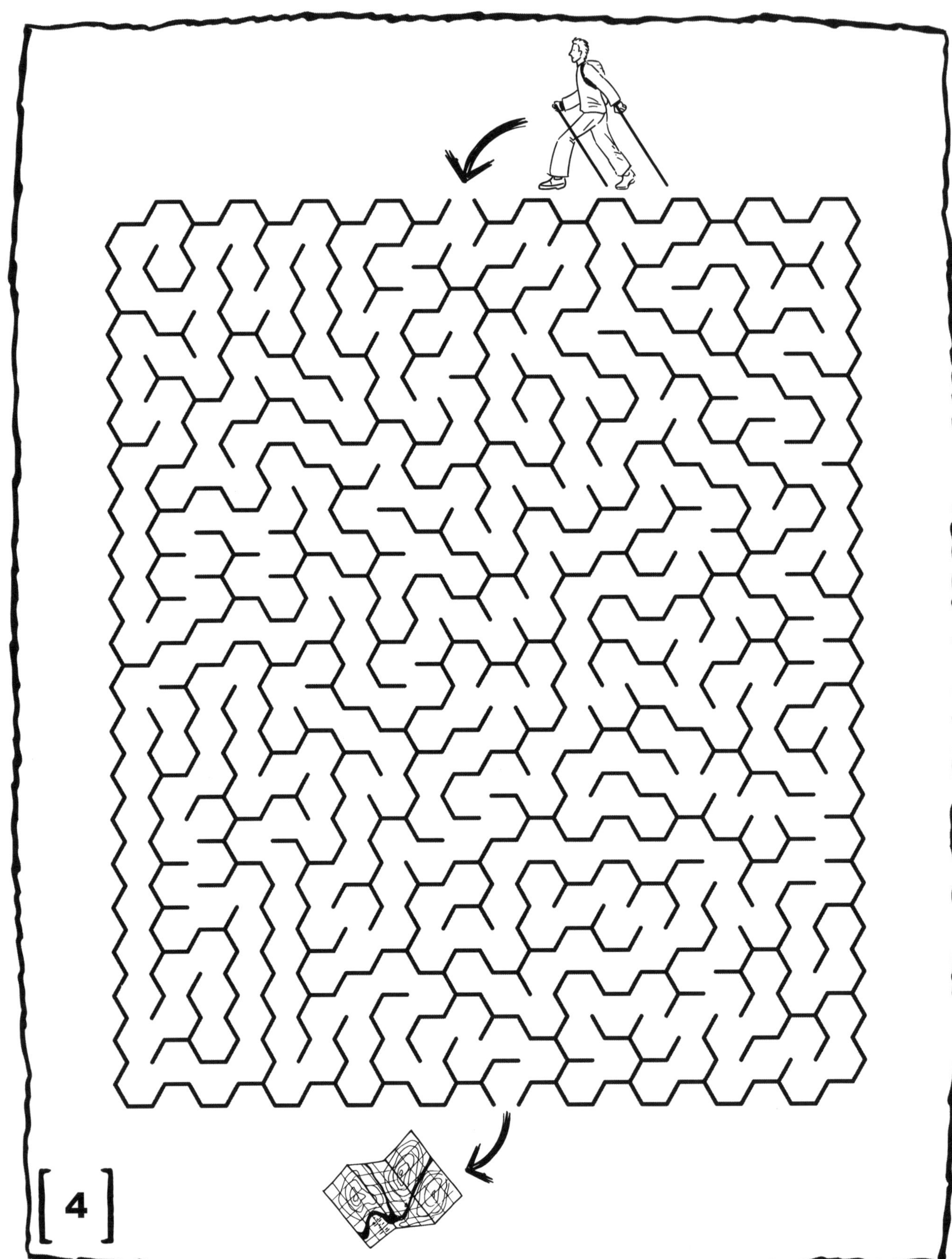

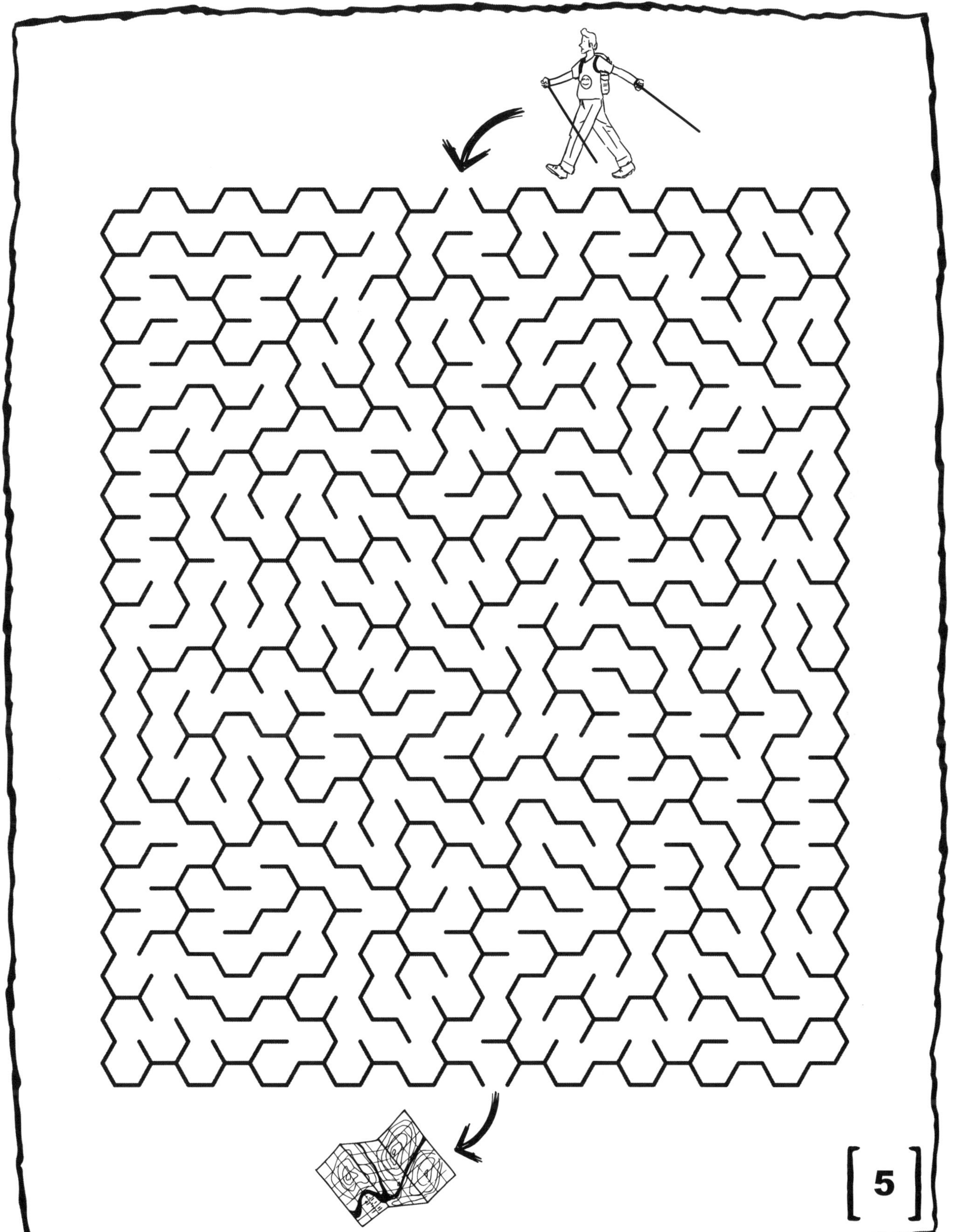

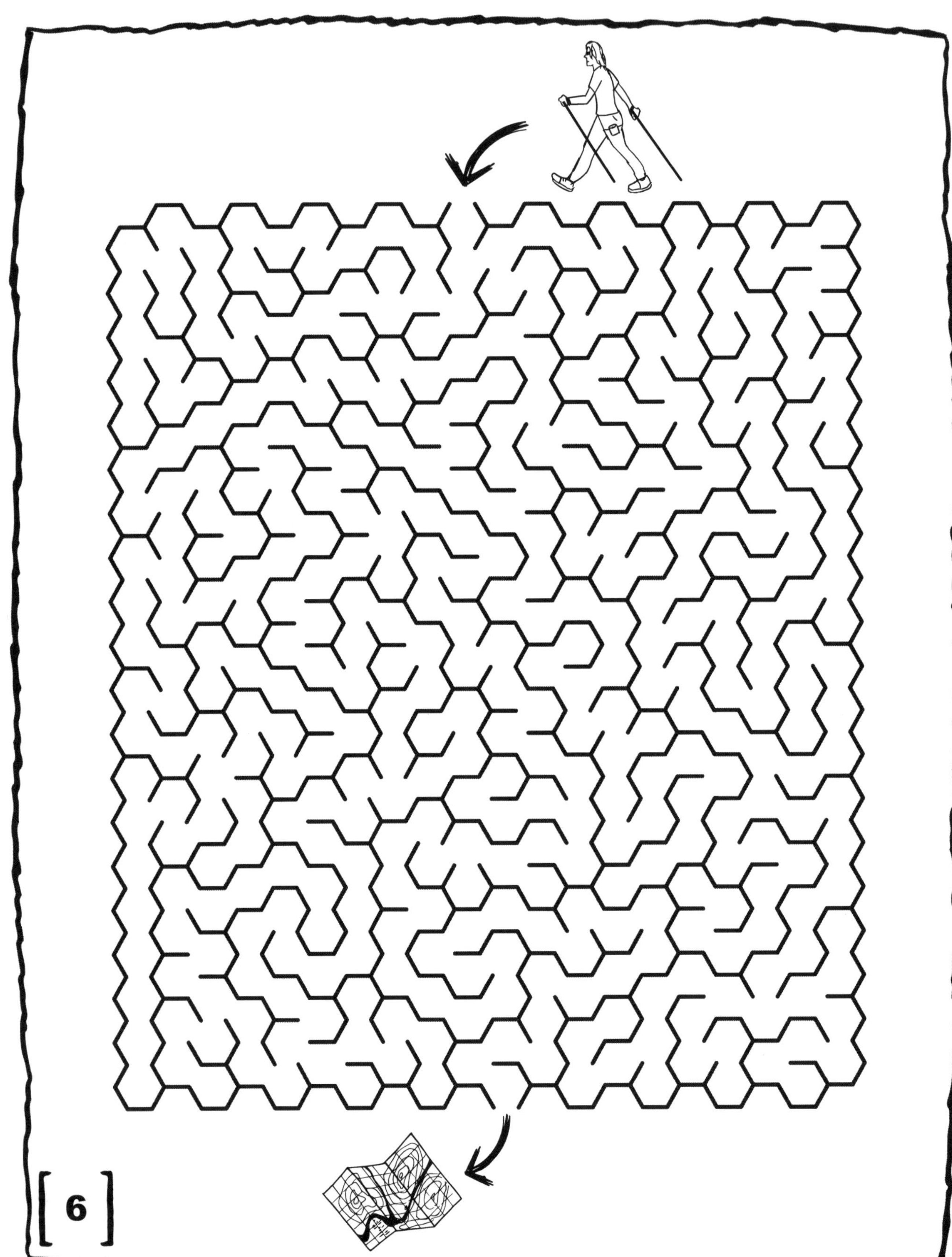

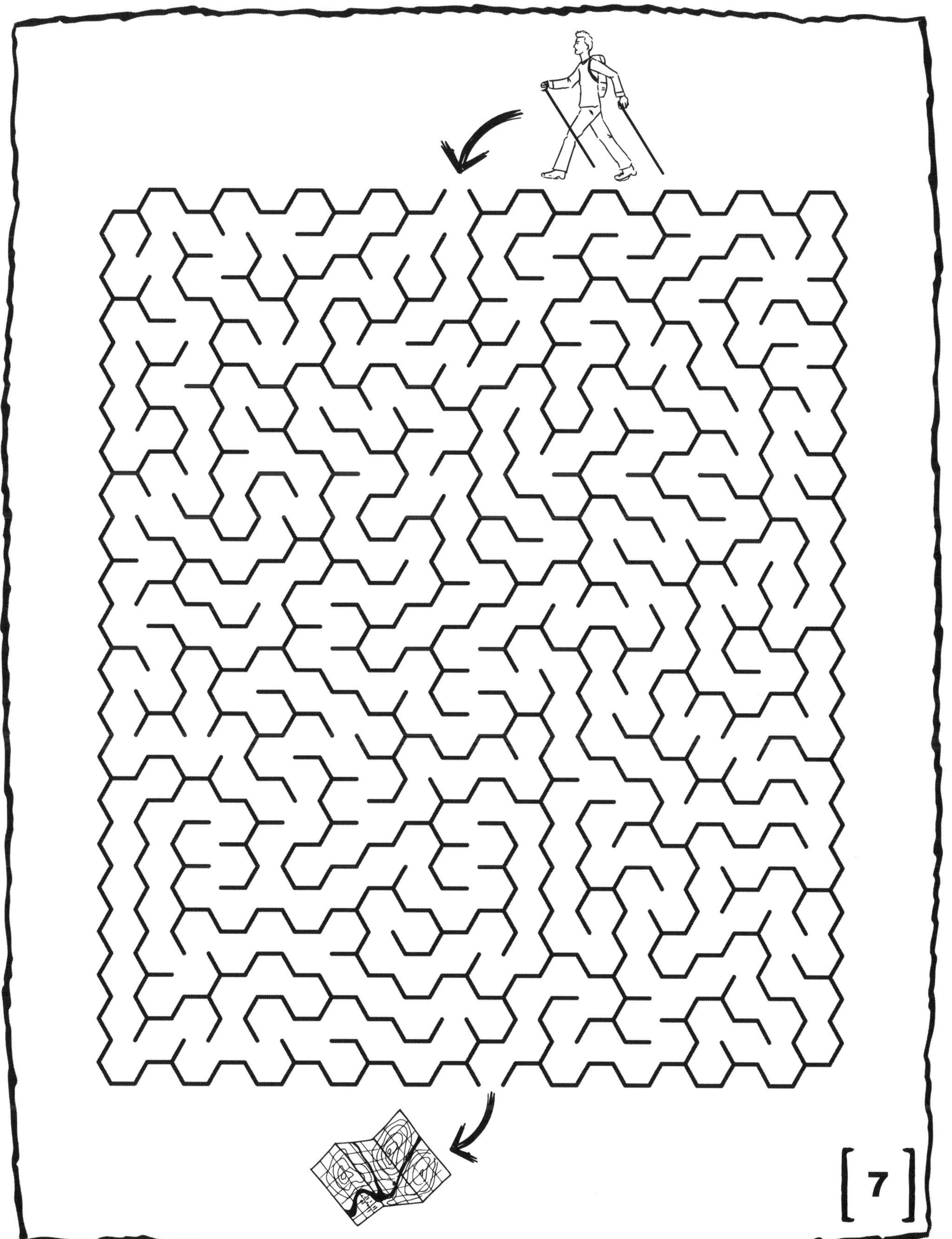

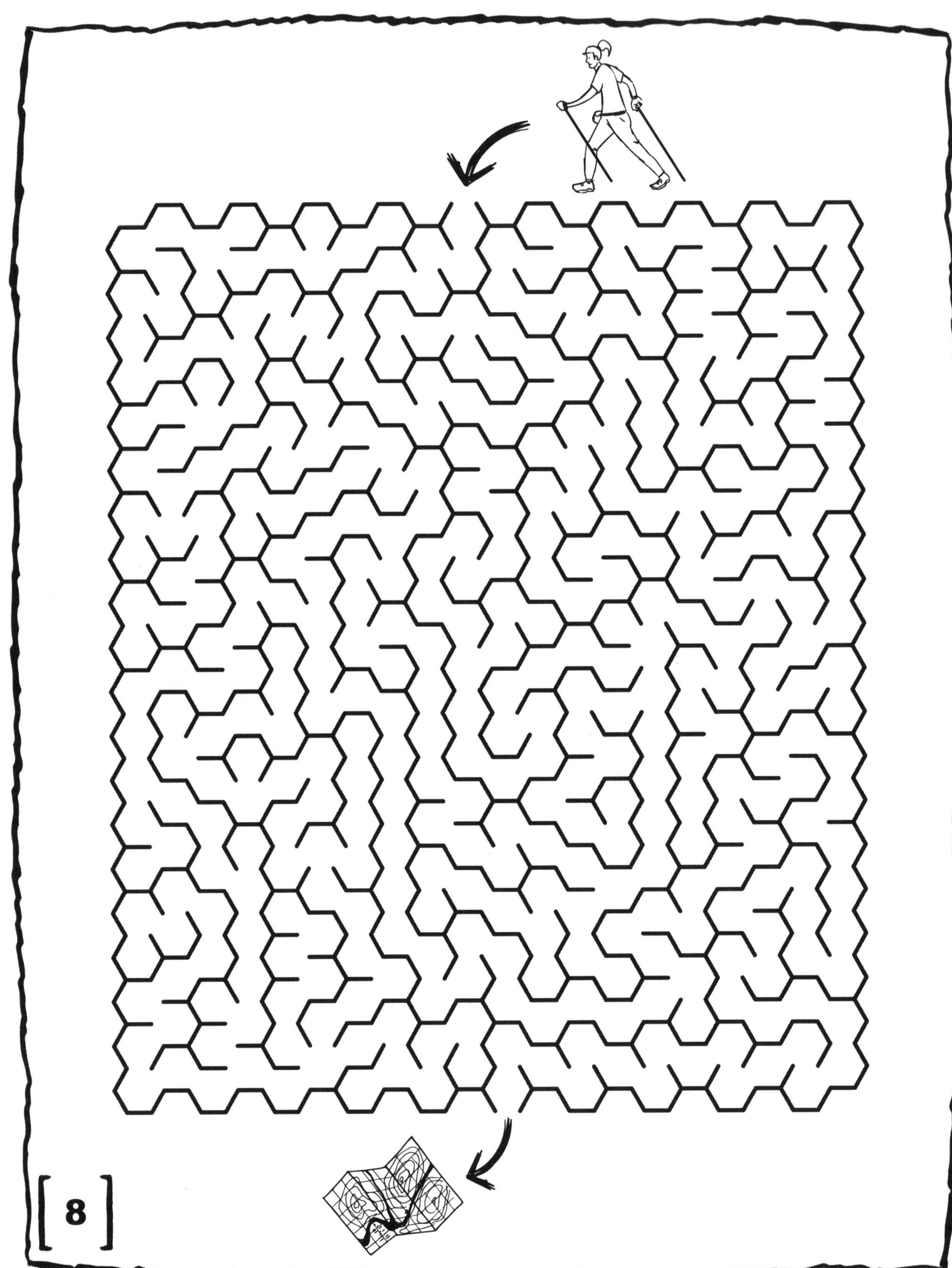

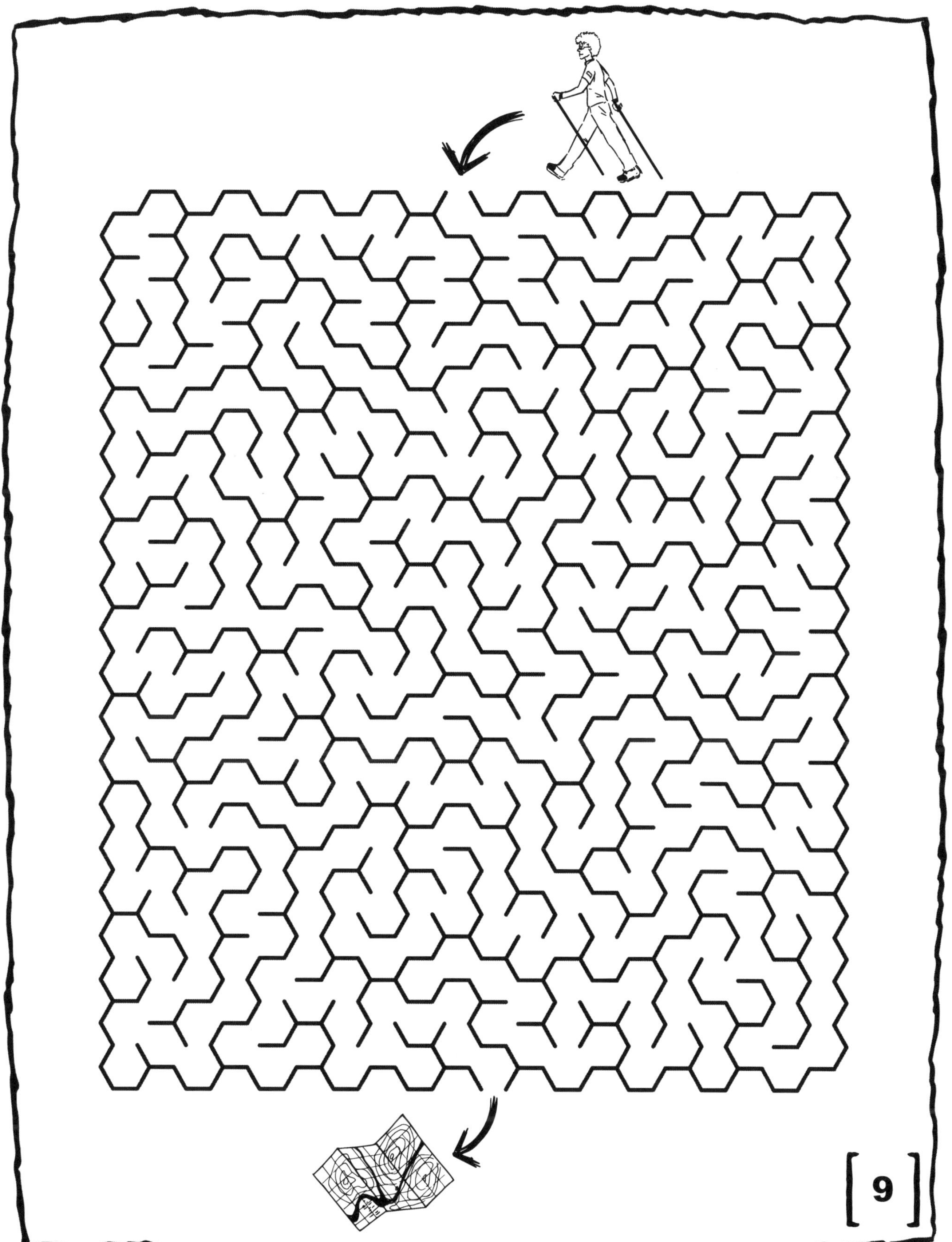

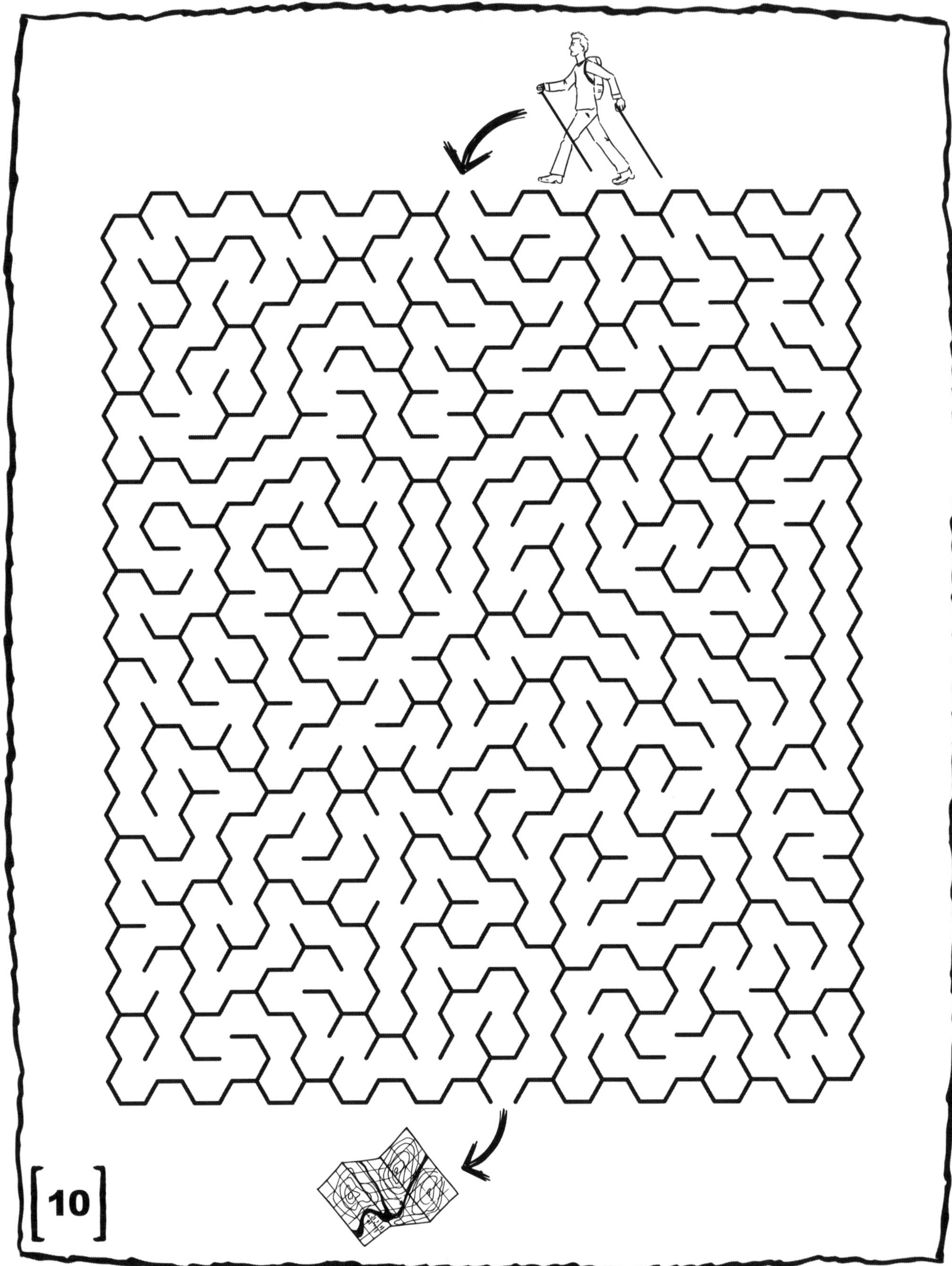

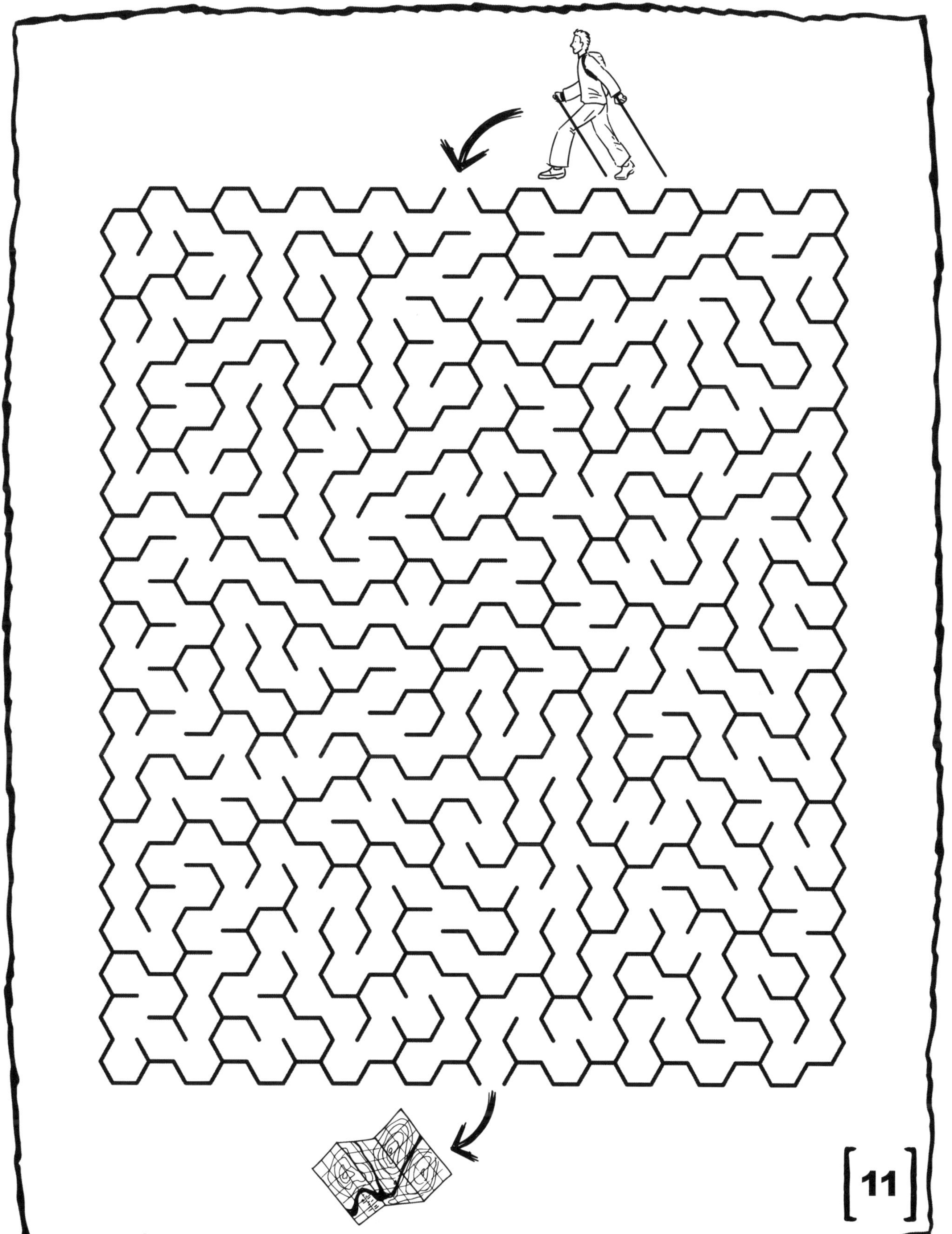

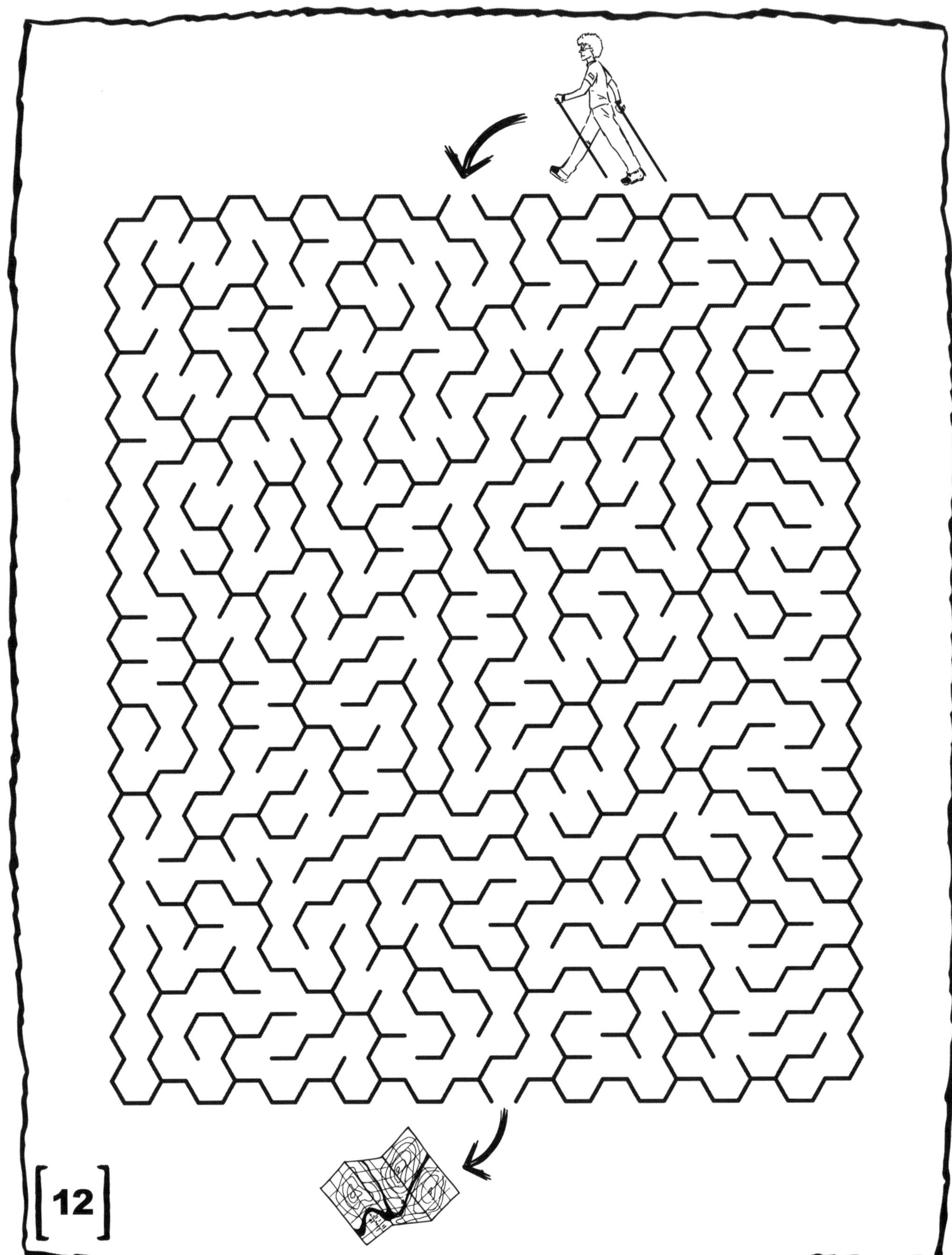

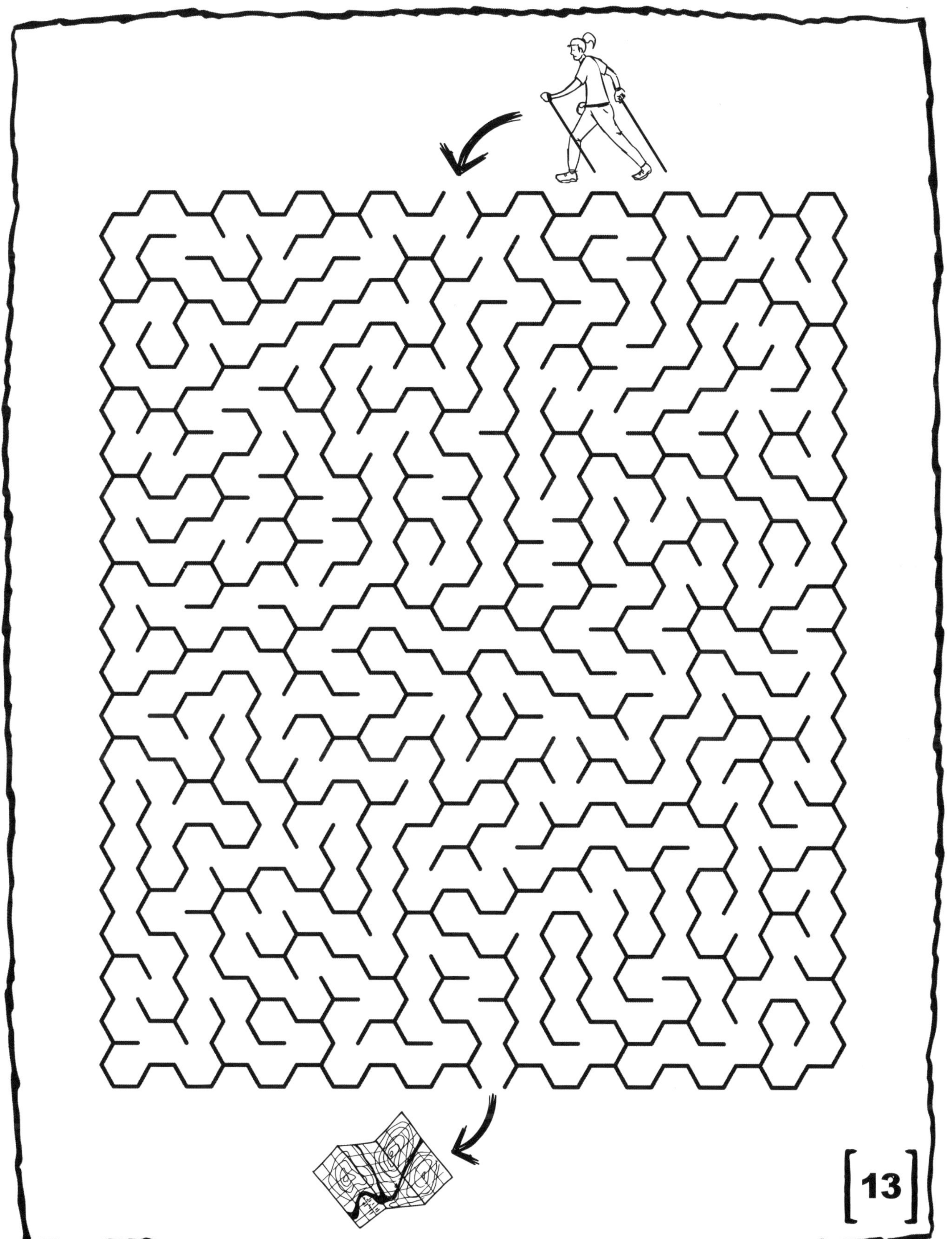

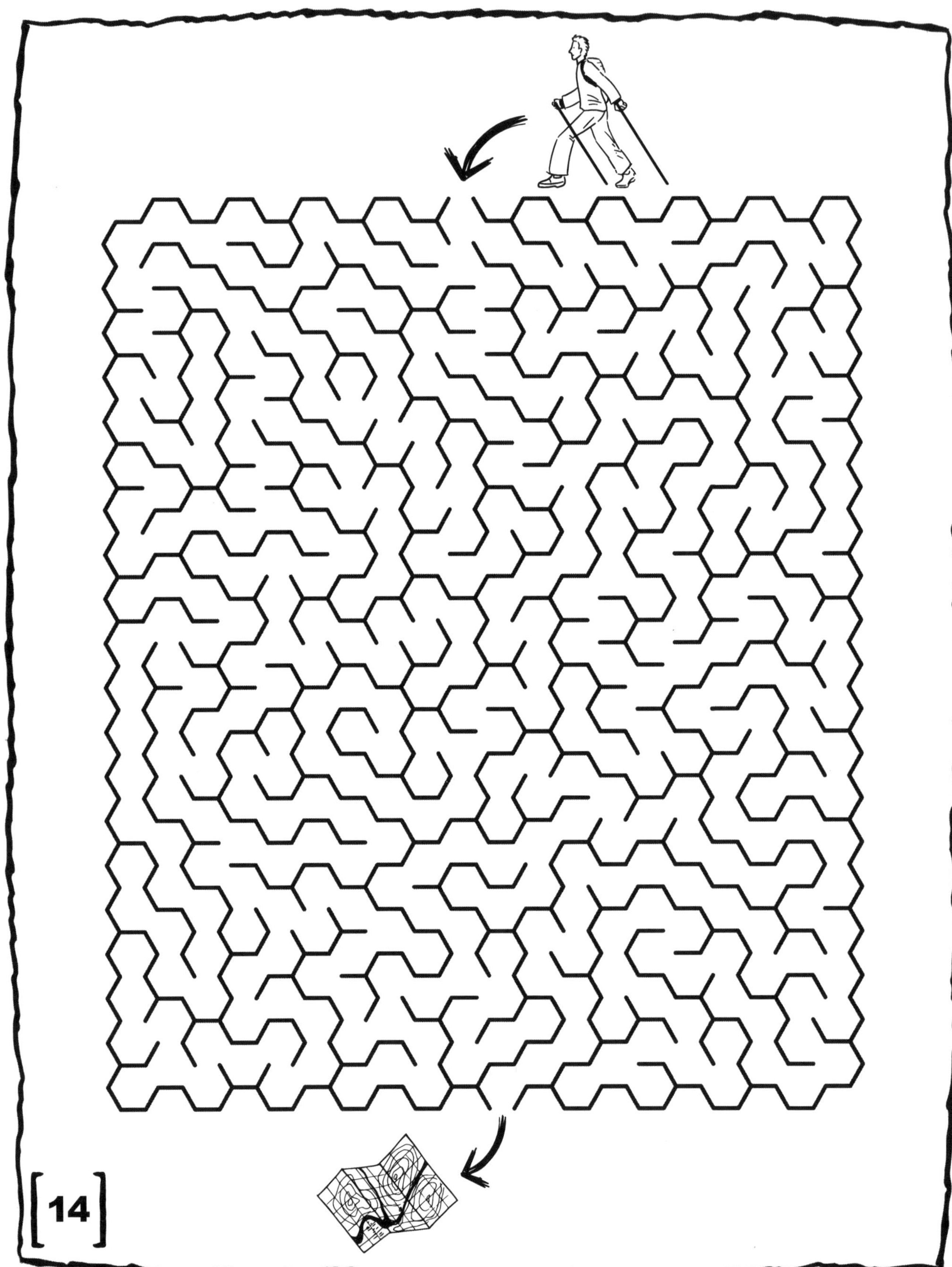

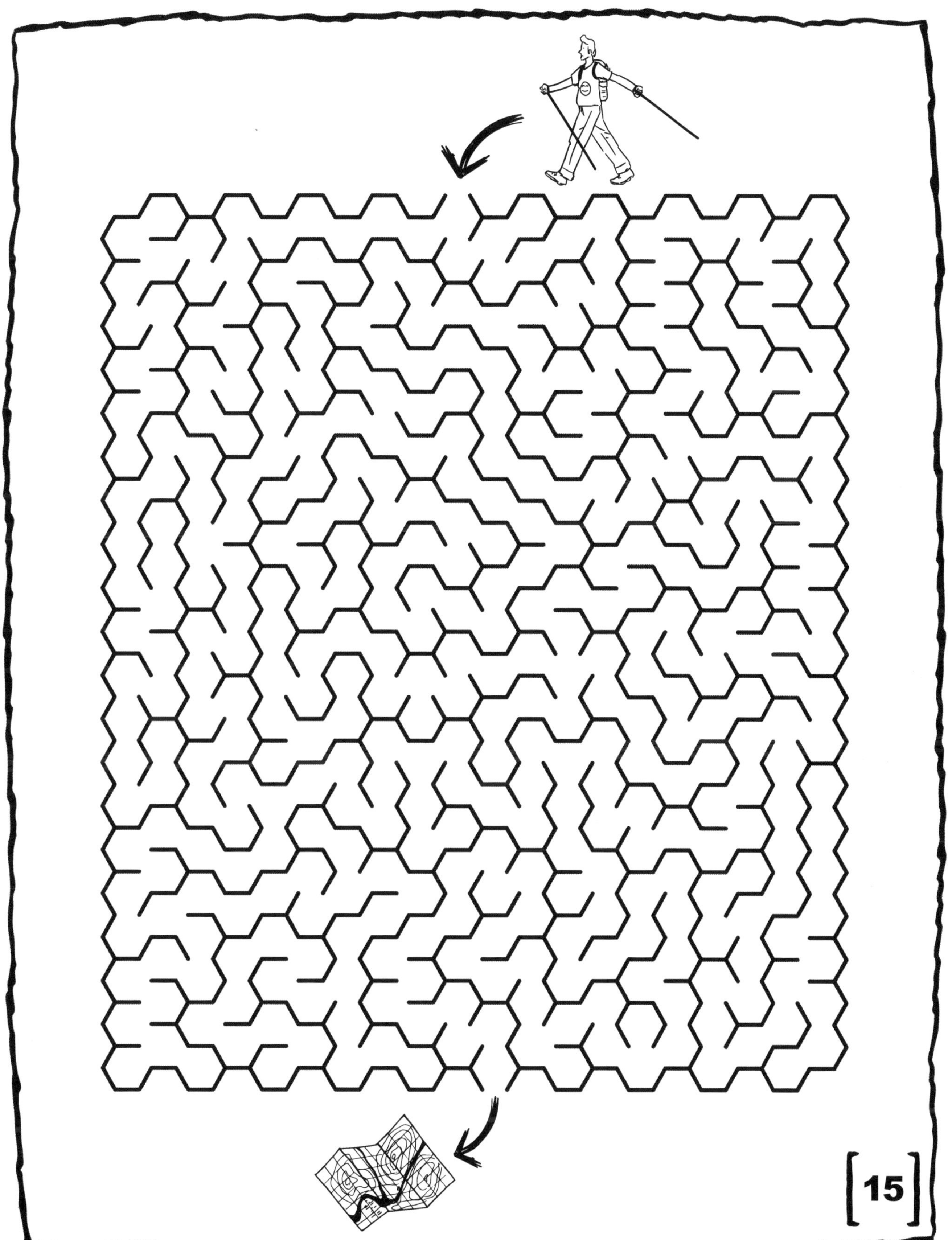

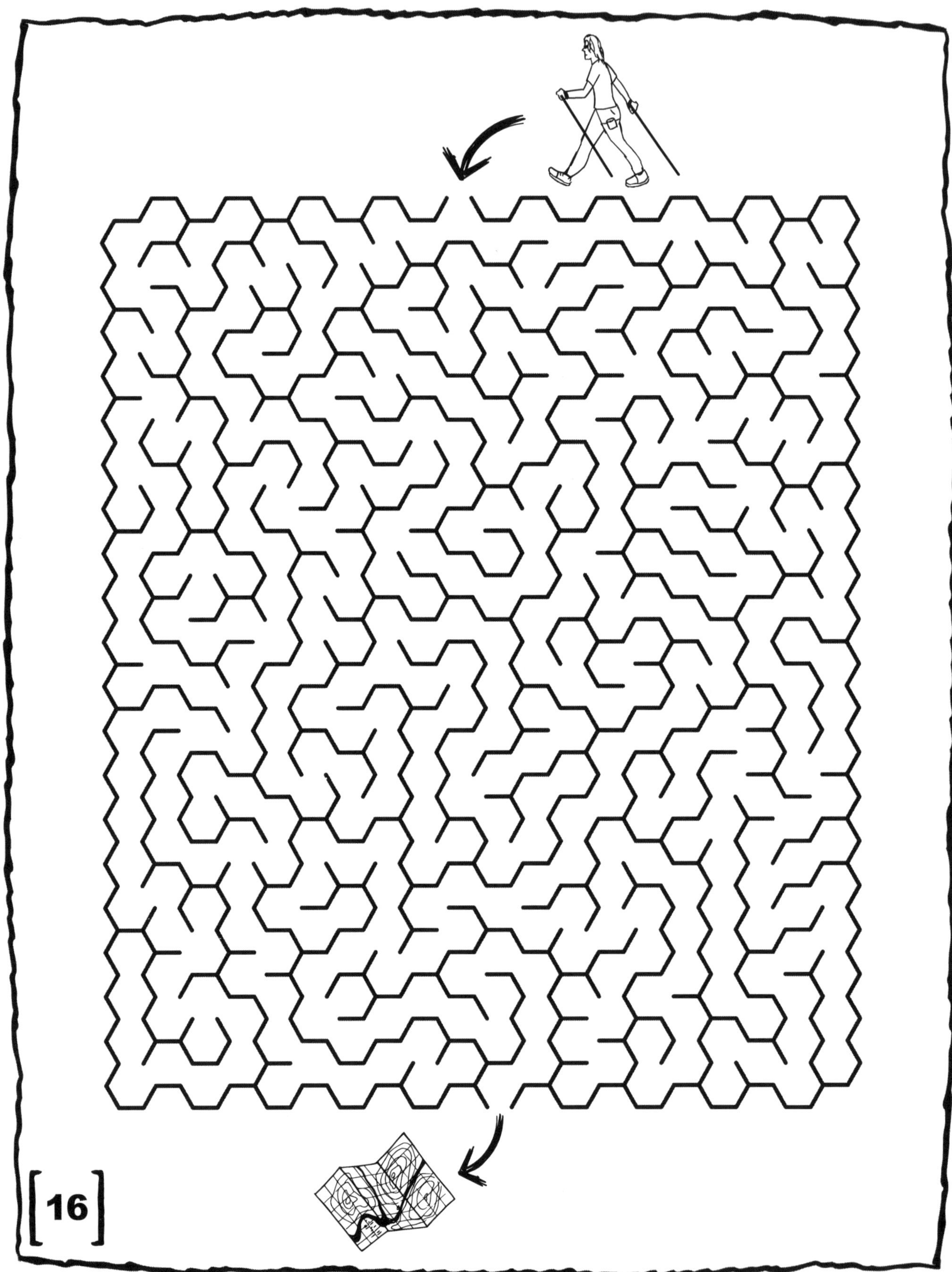

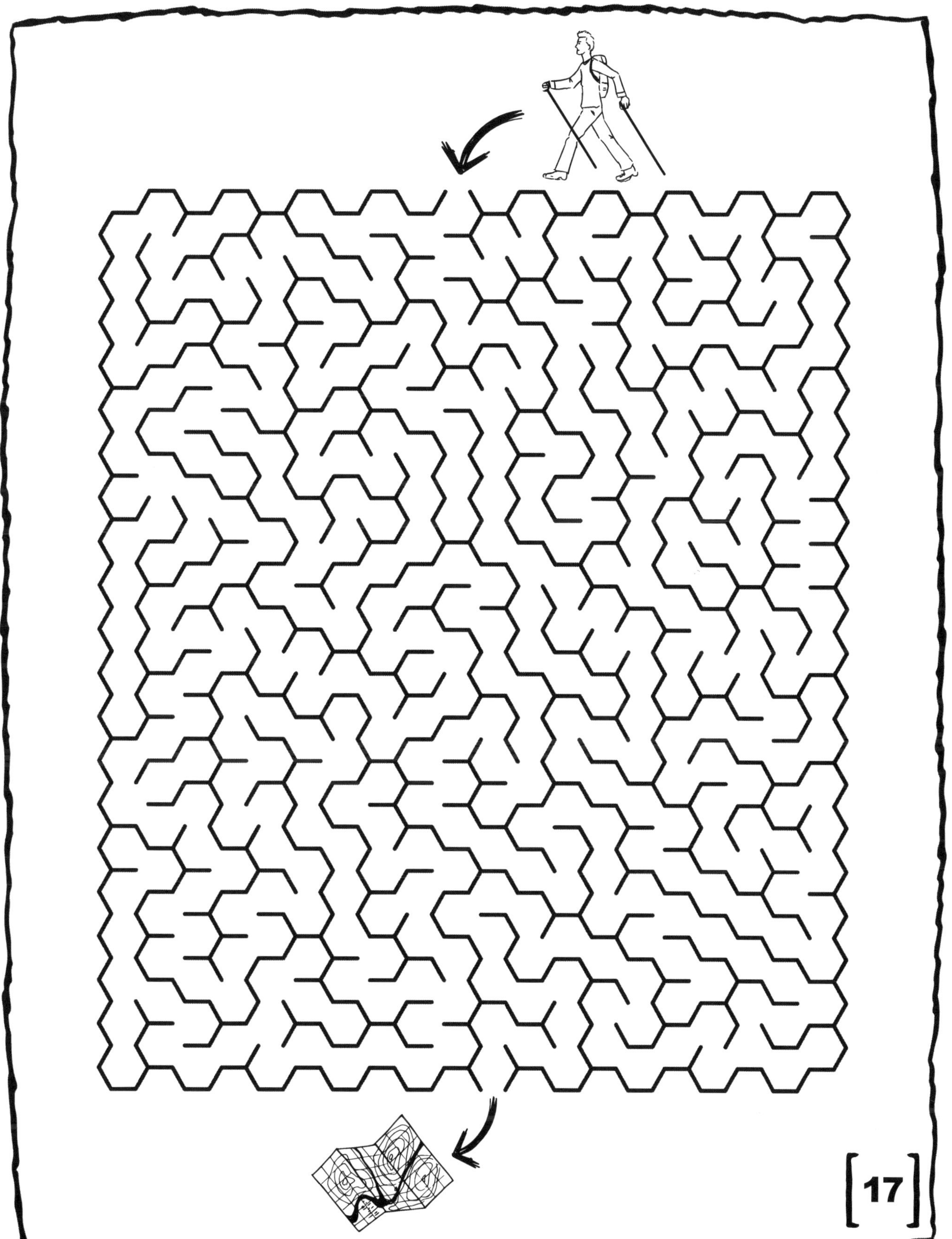

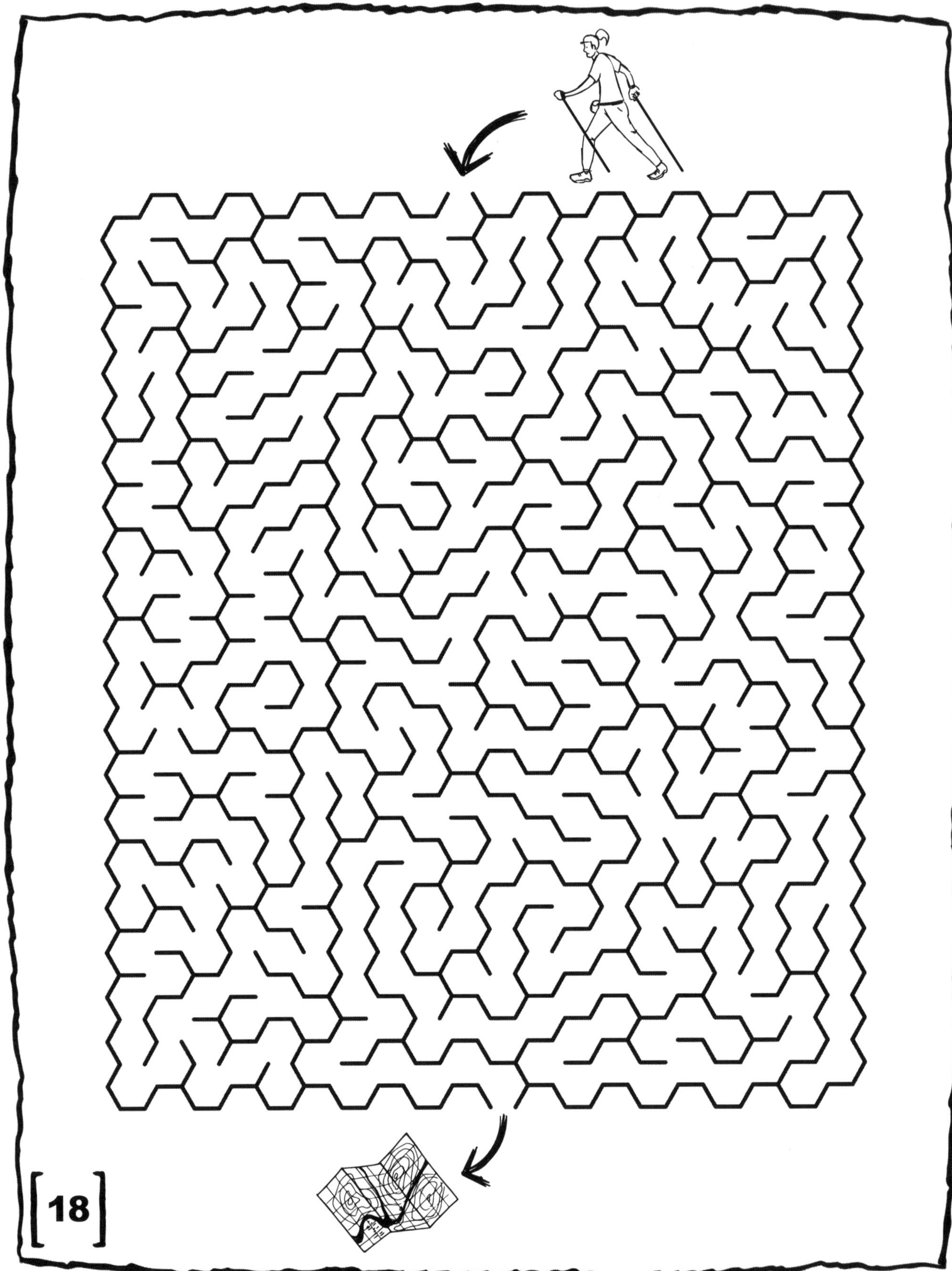

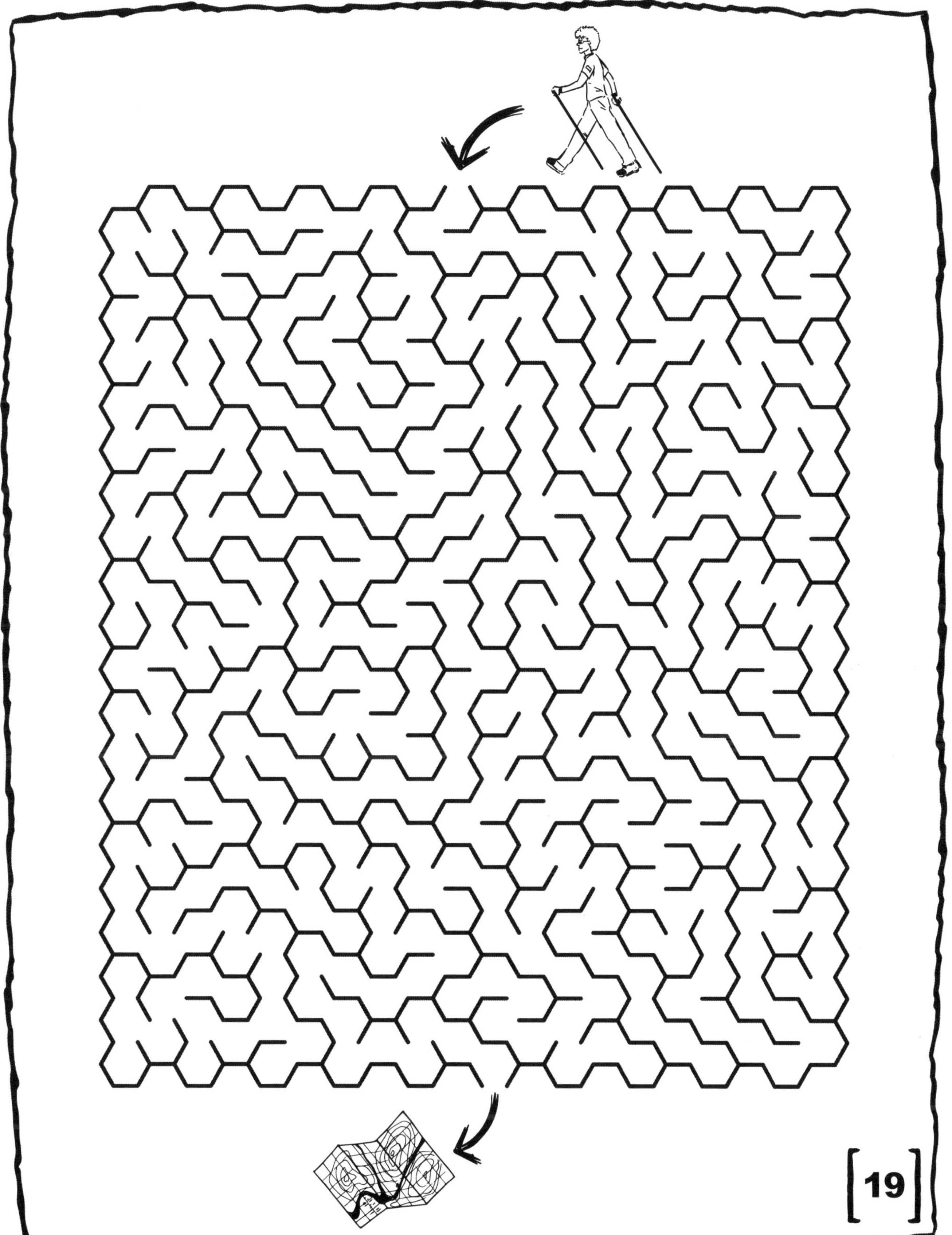

19

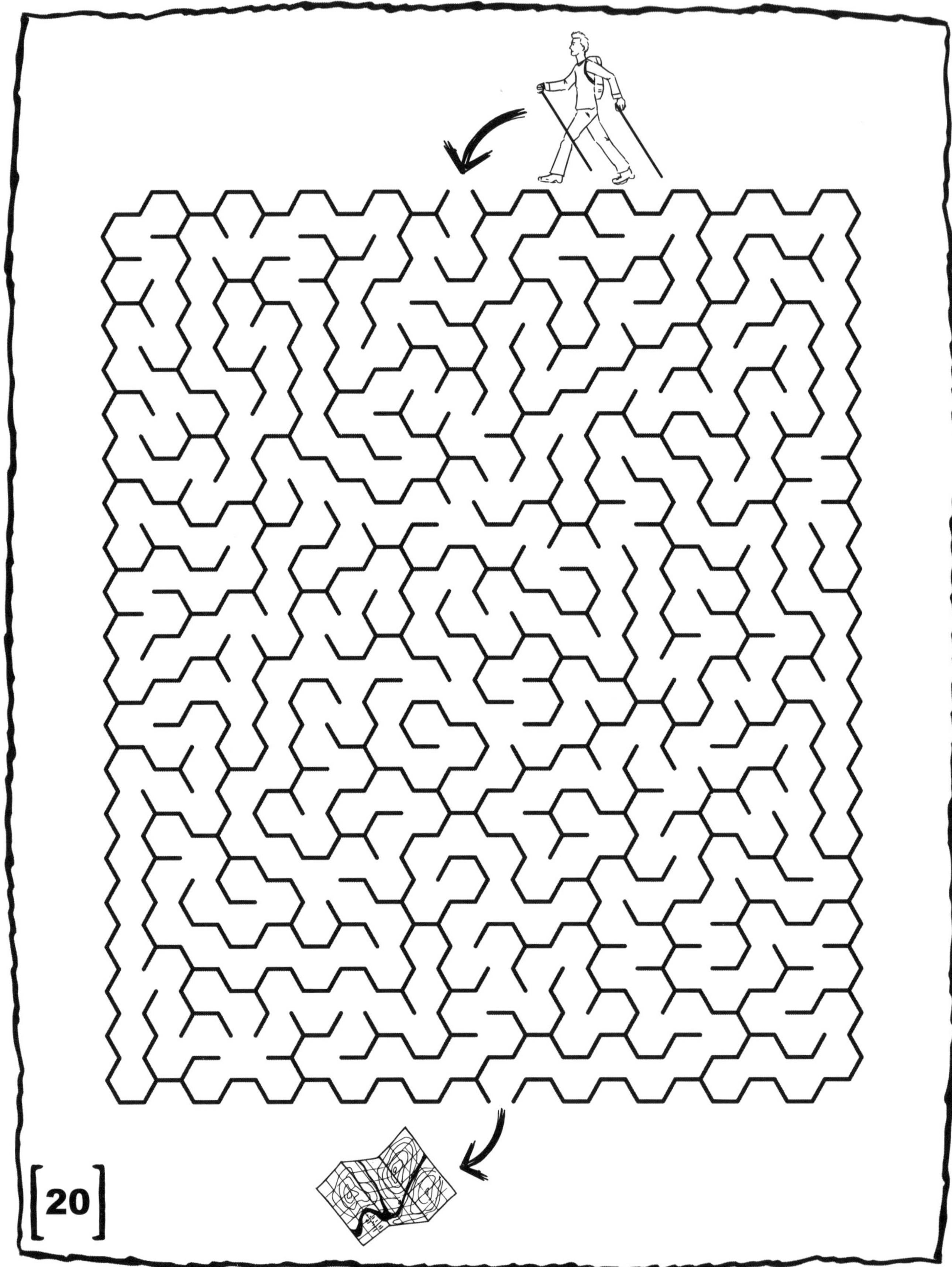

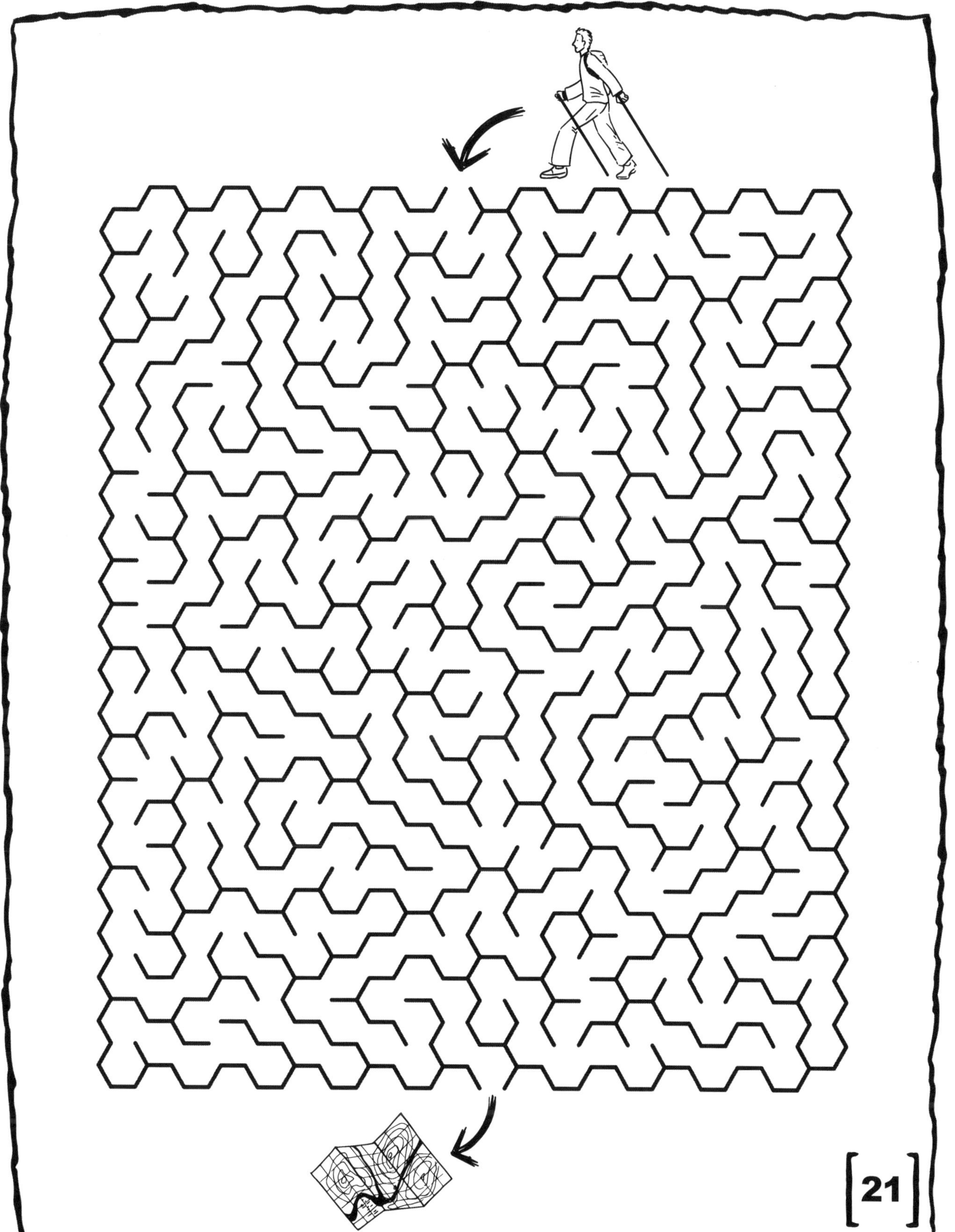

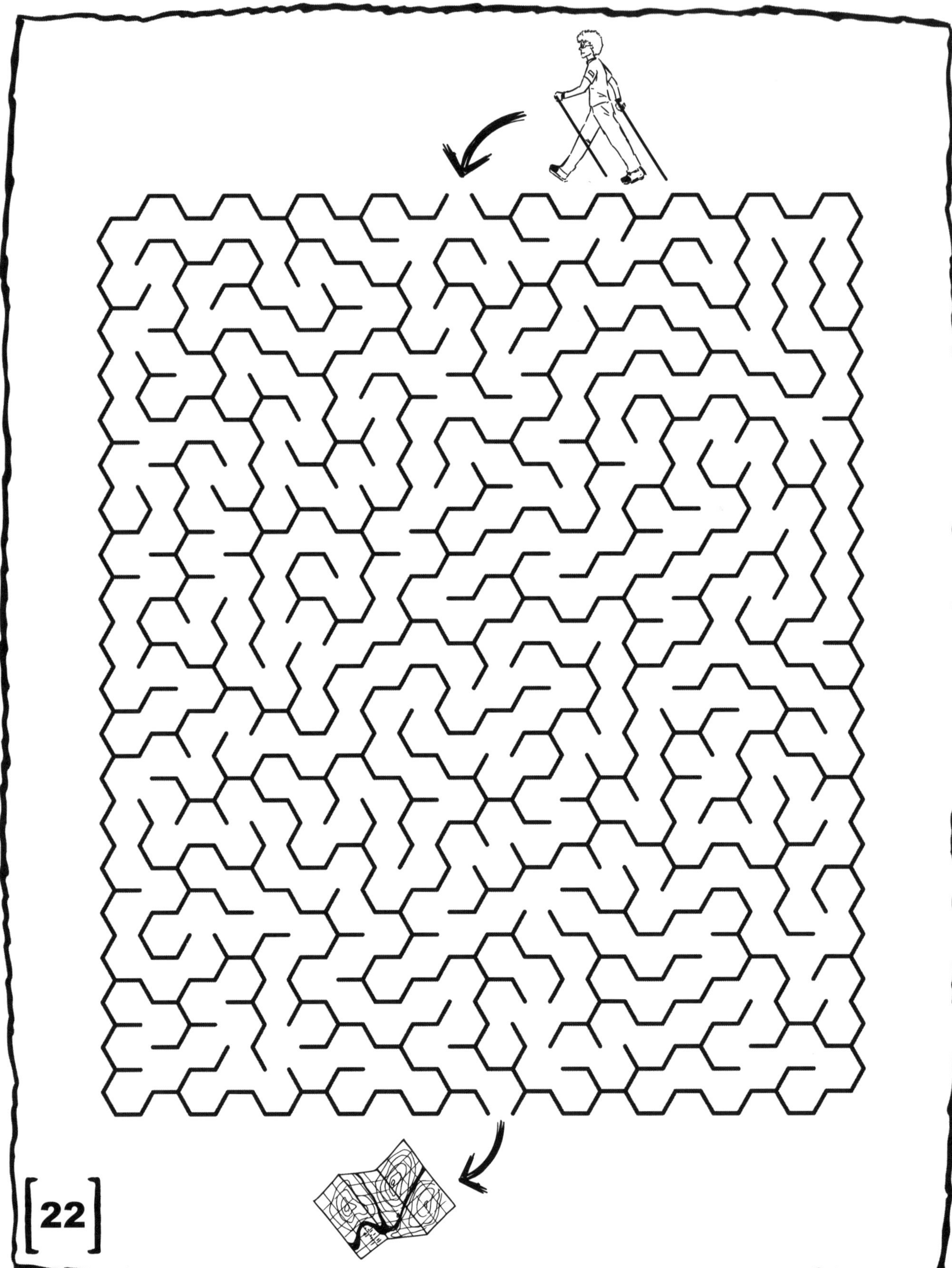

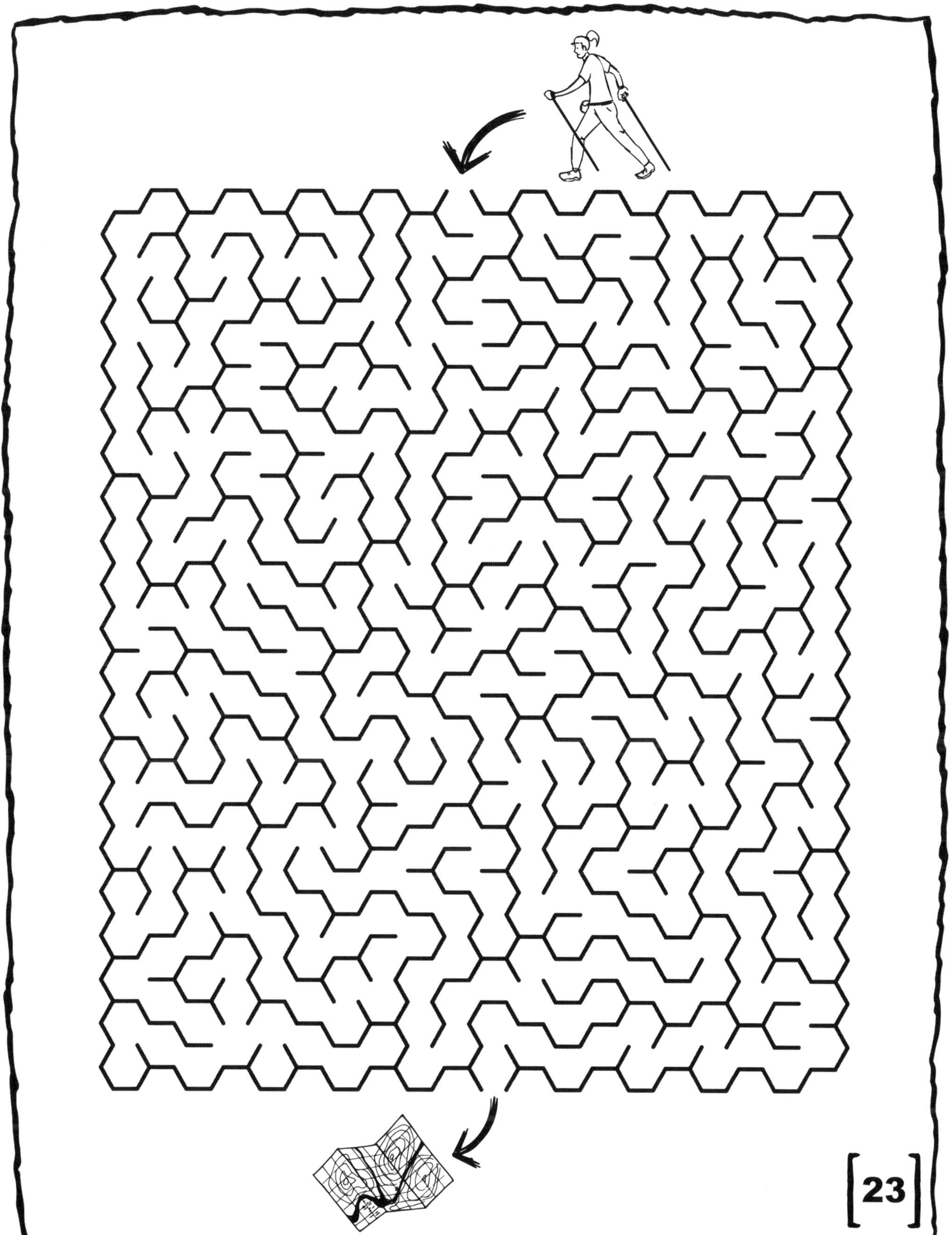

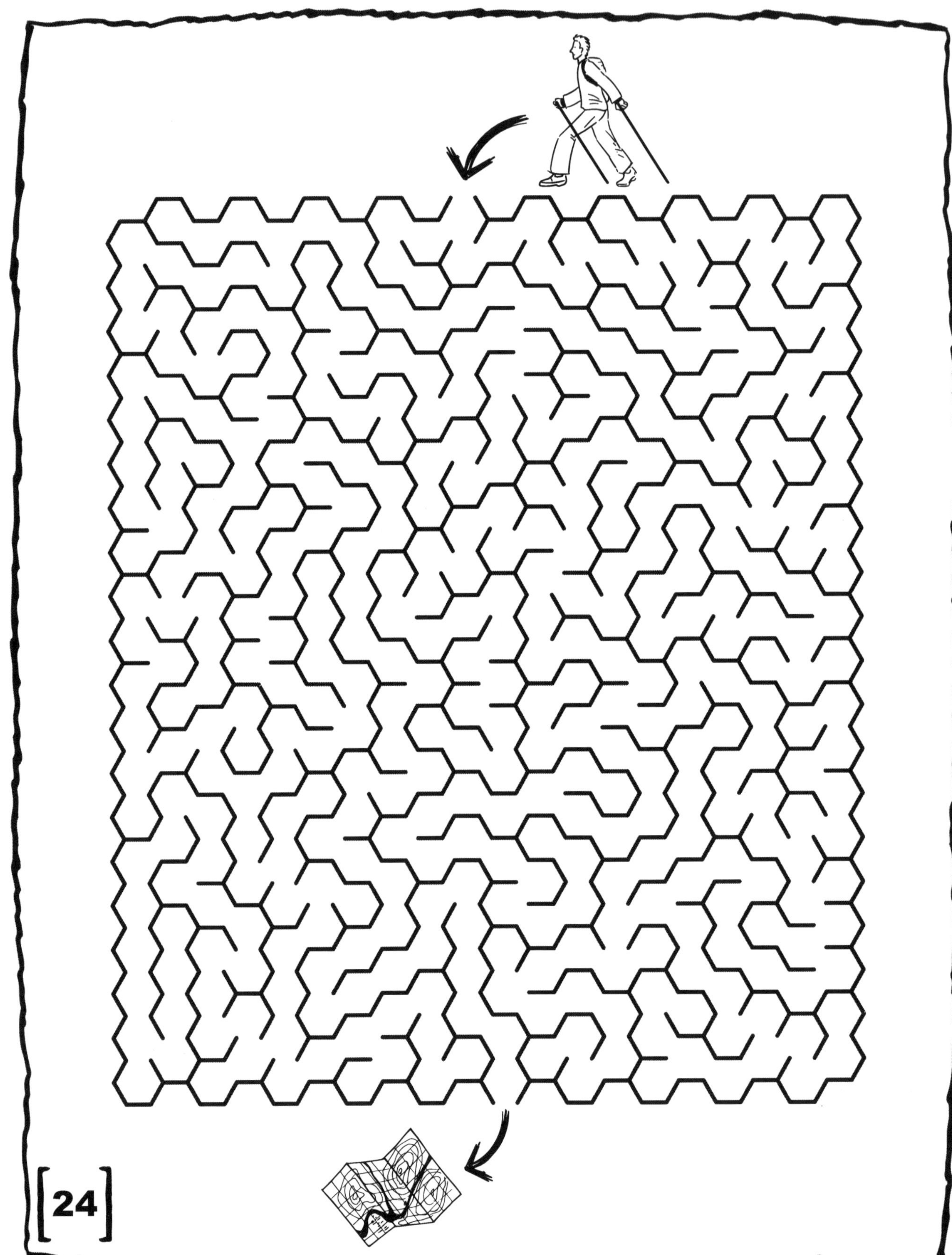

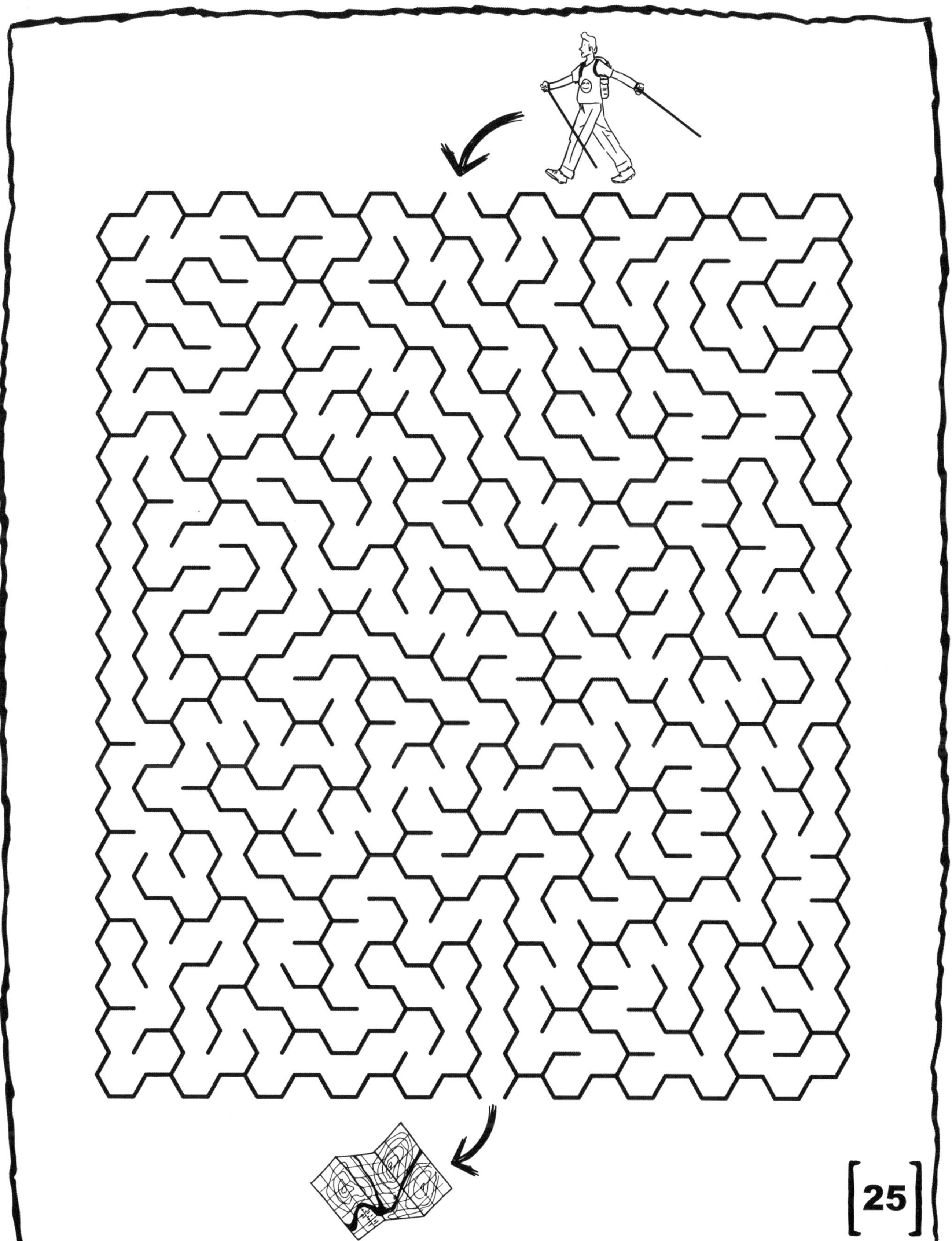

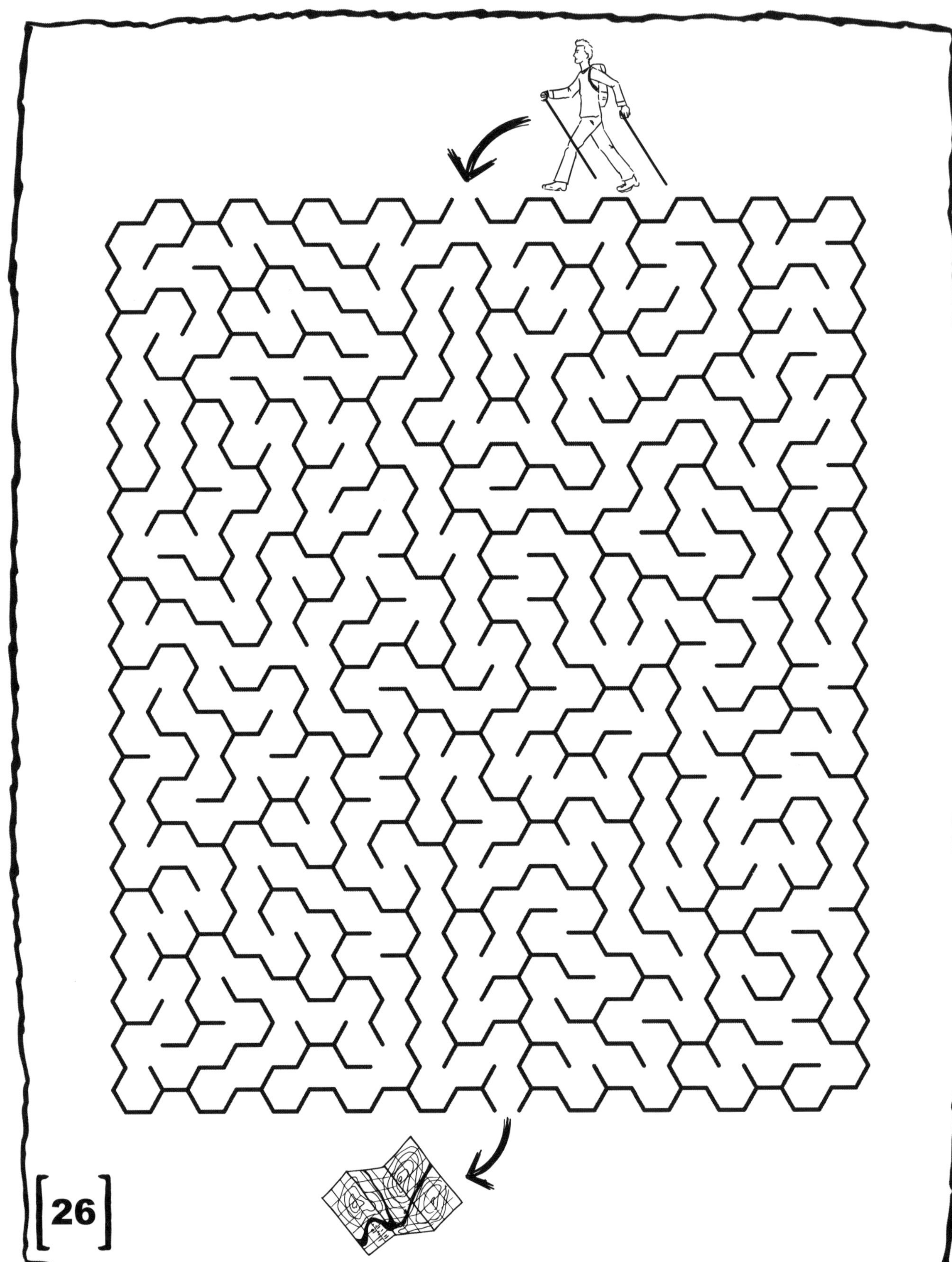

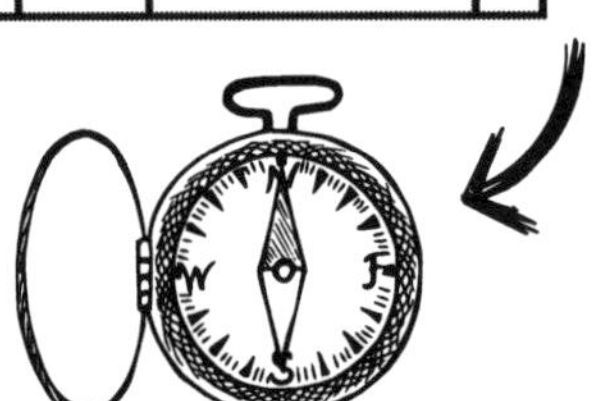

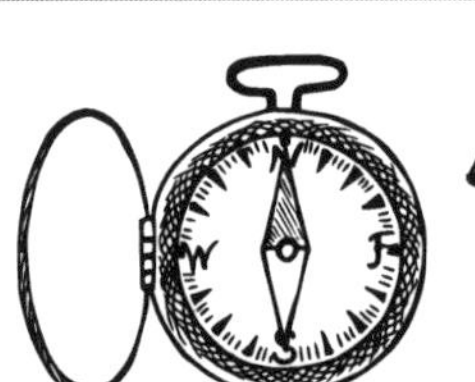

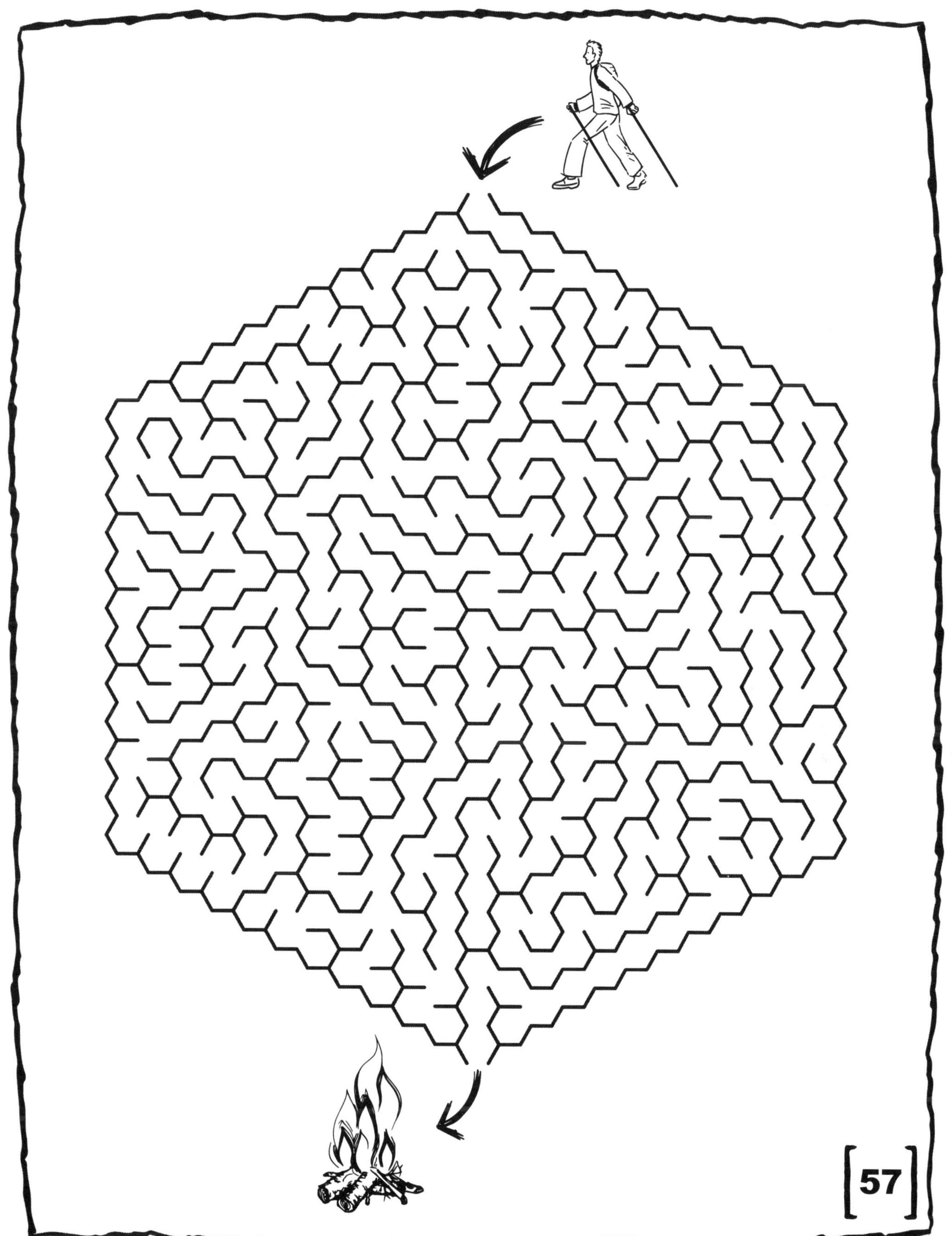

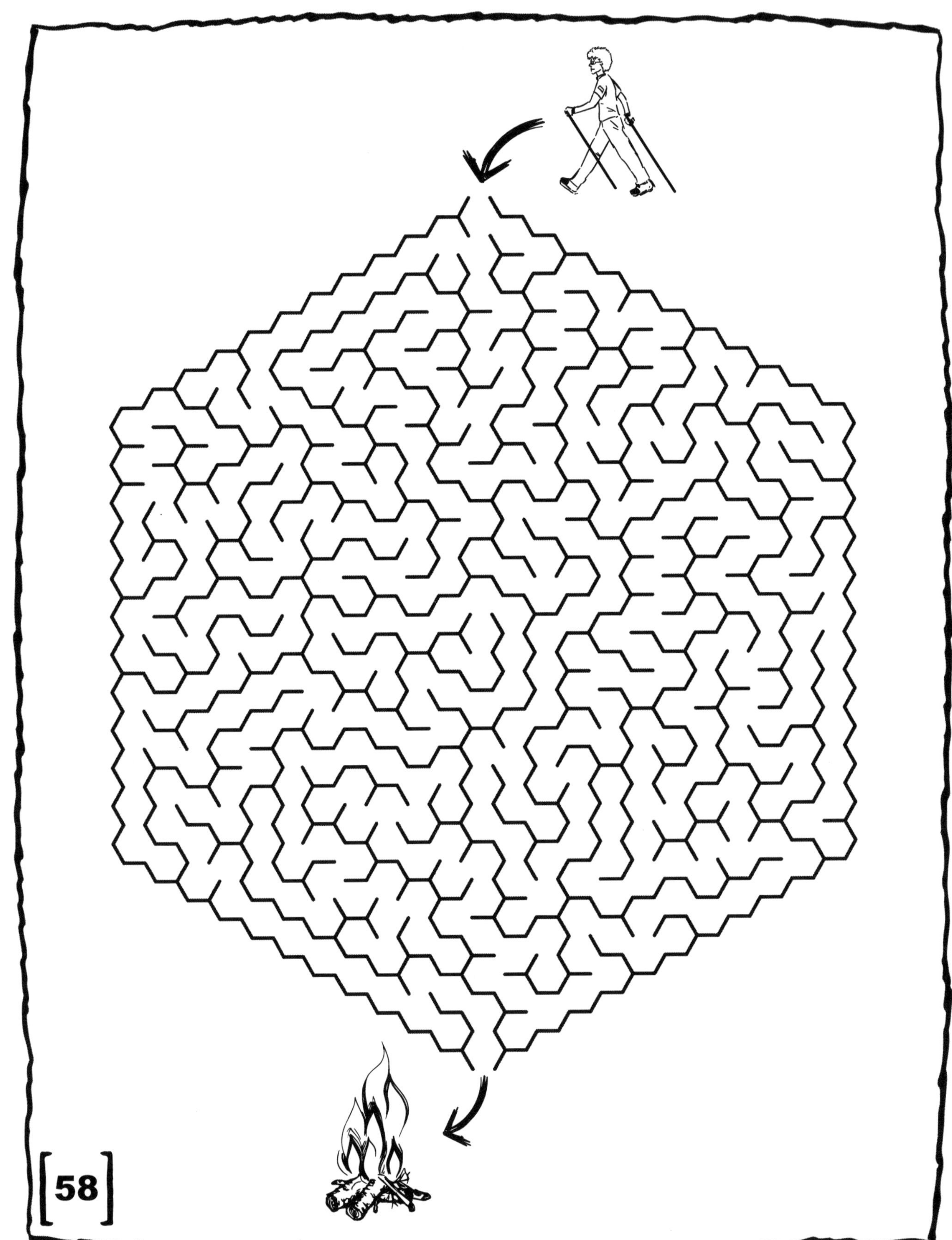

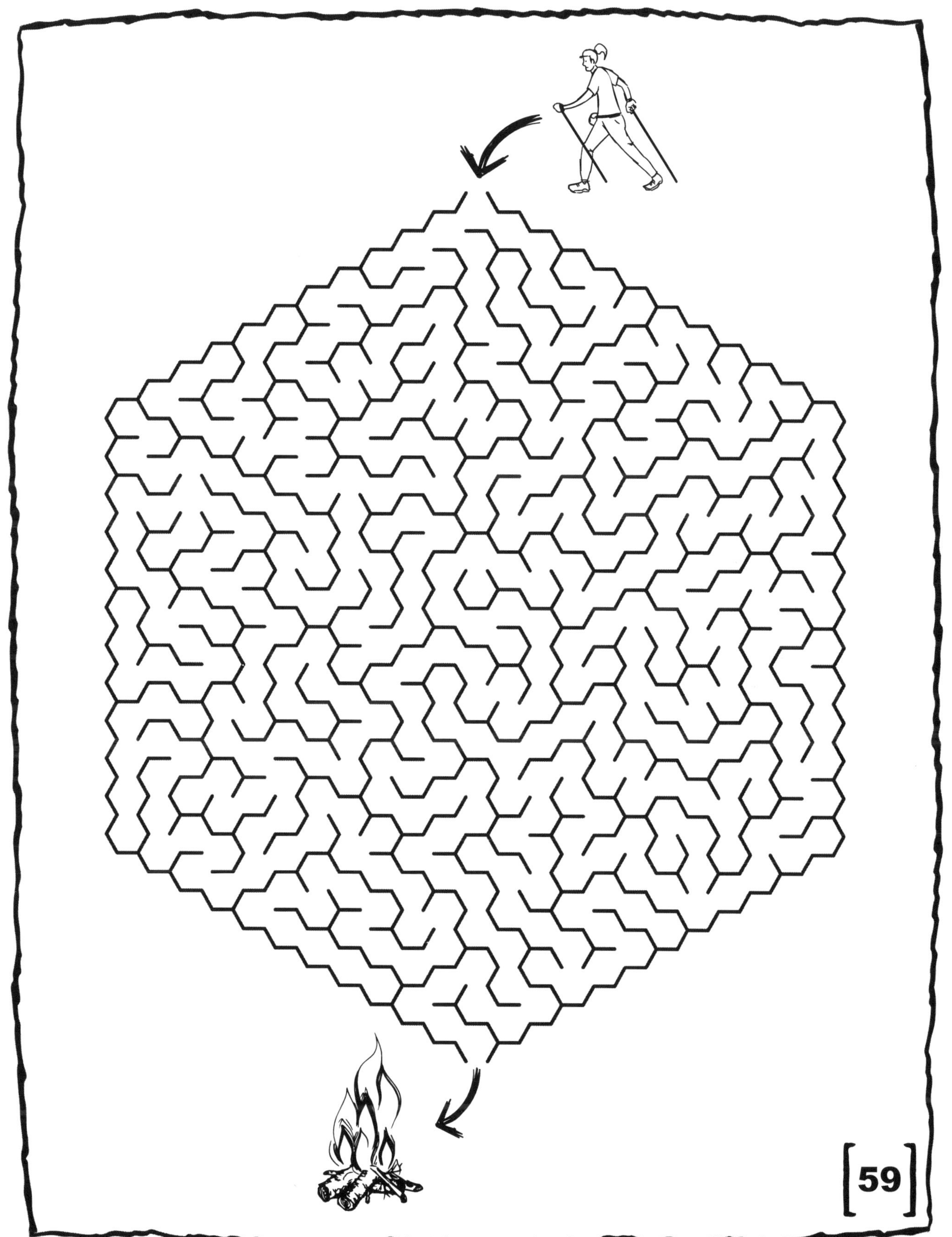

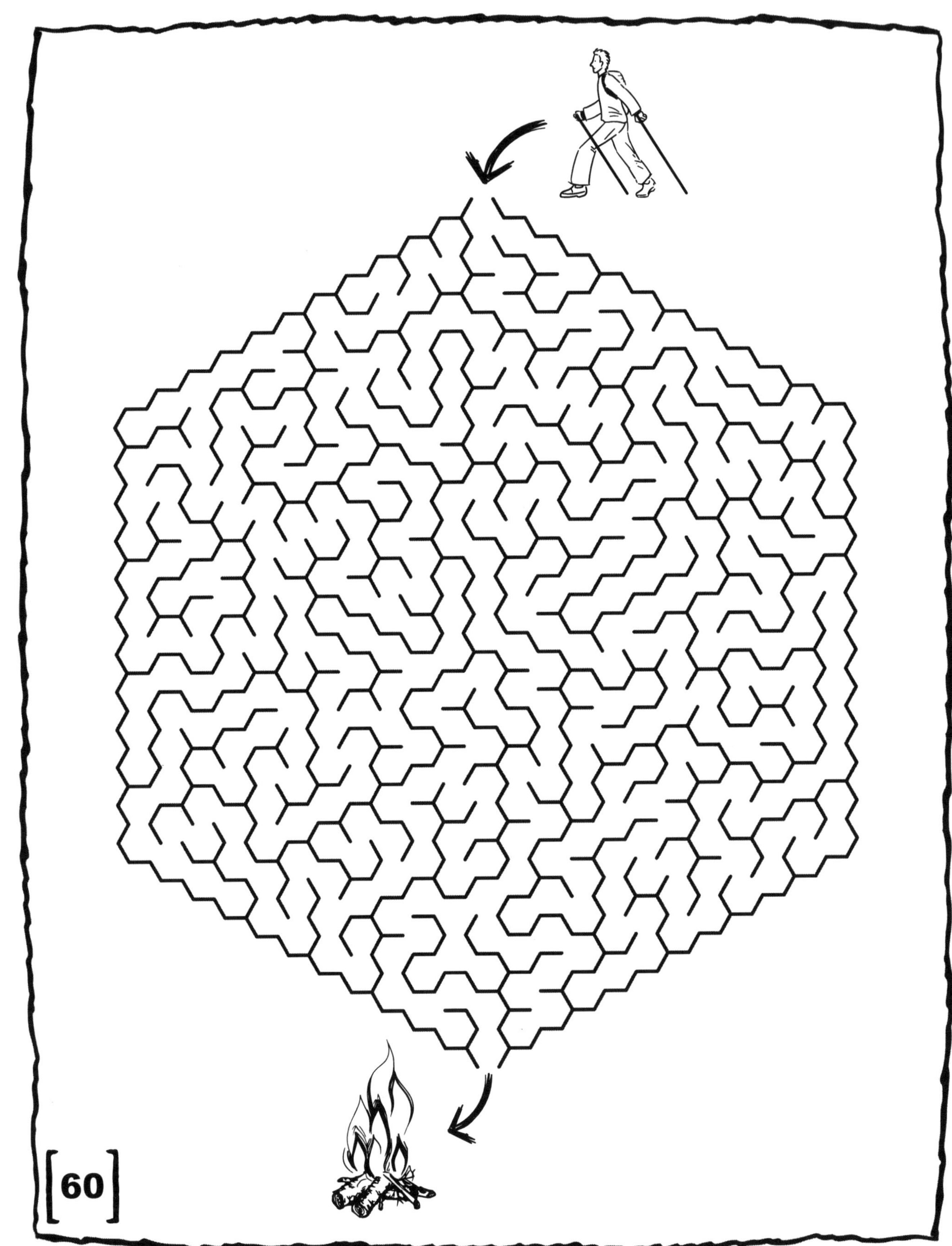

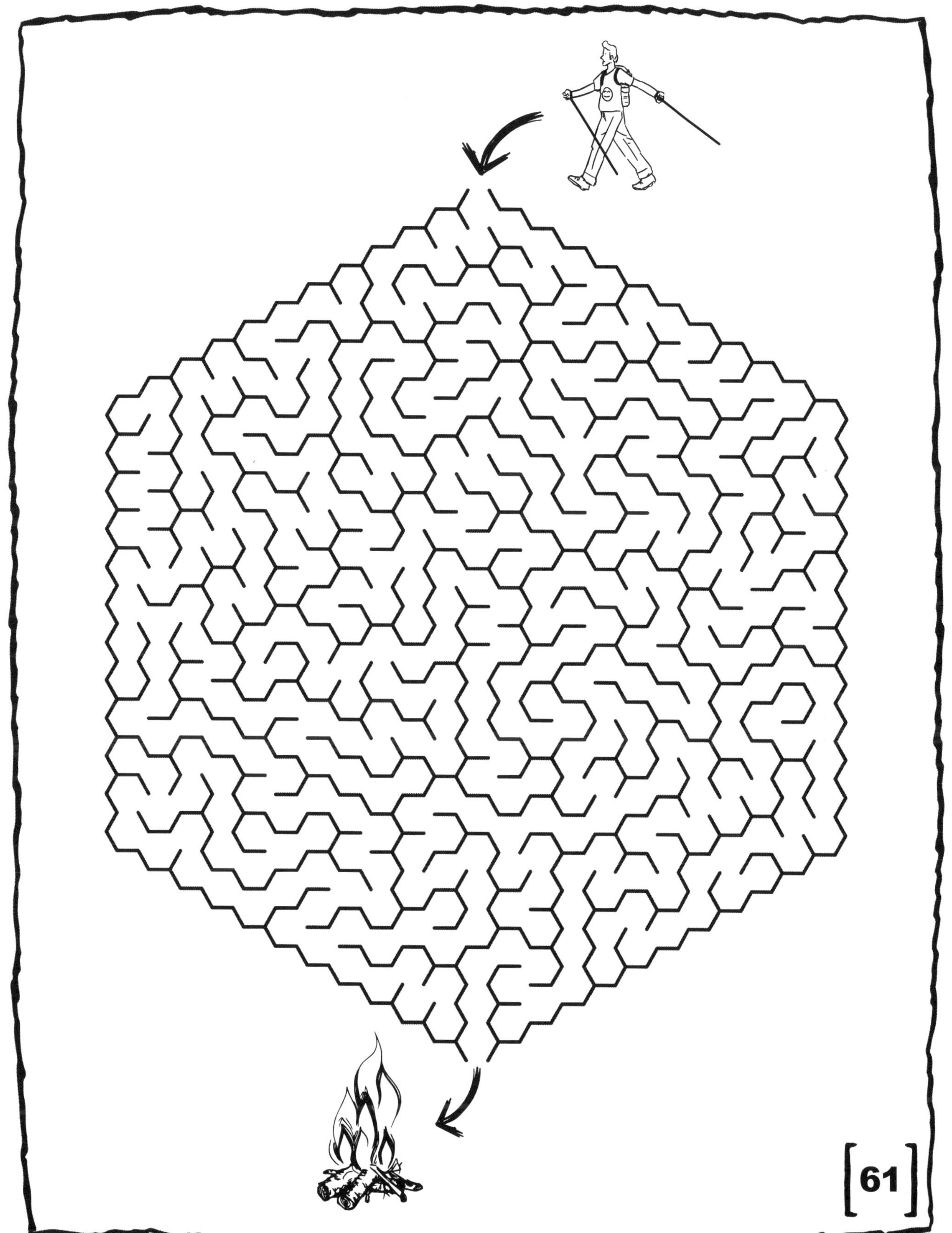

61

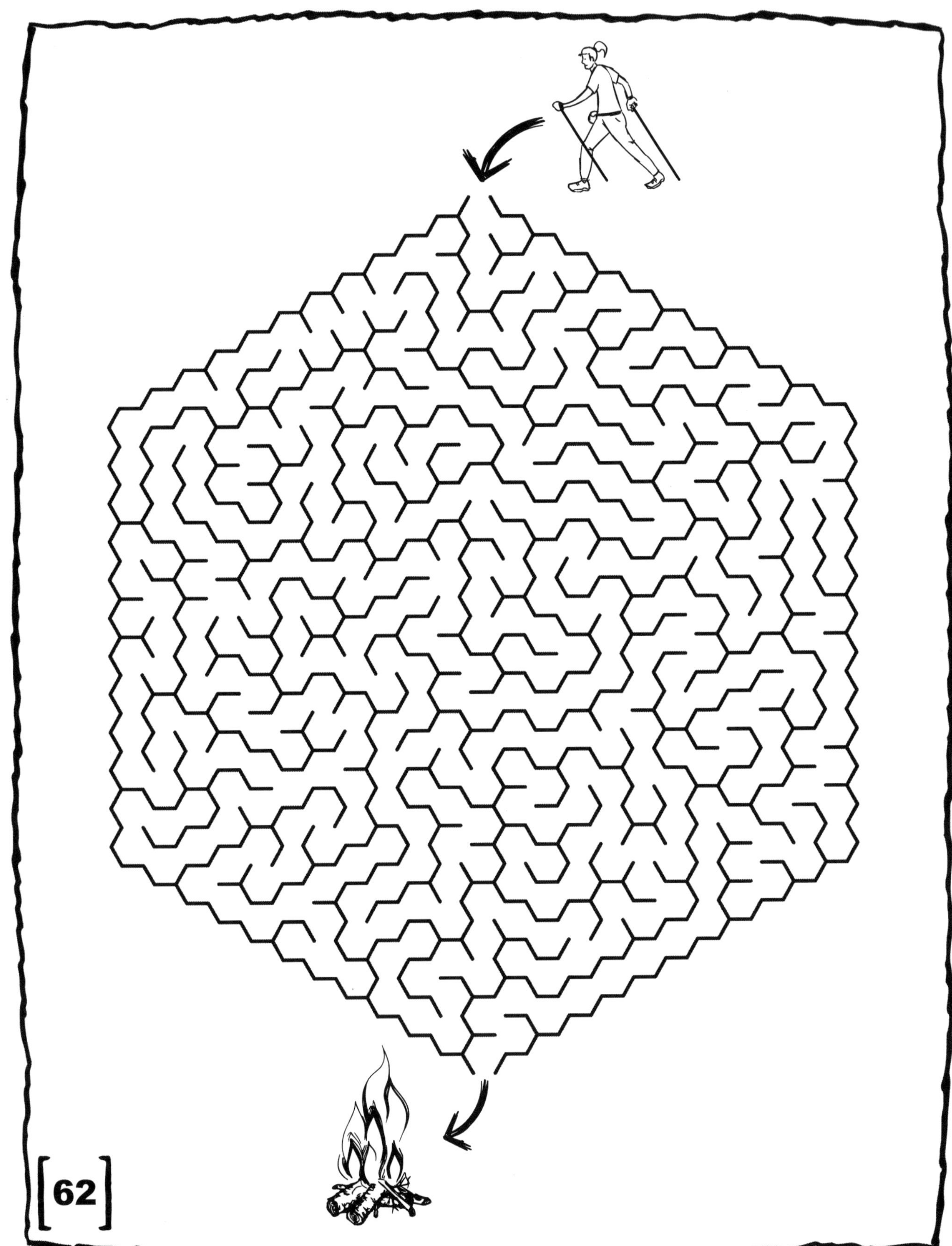

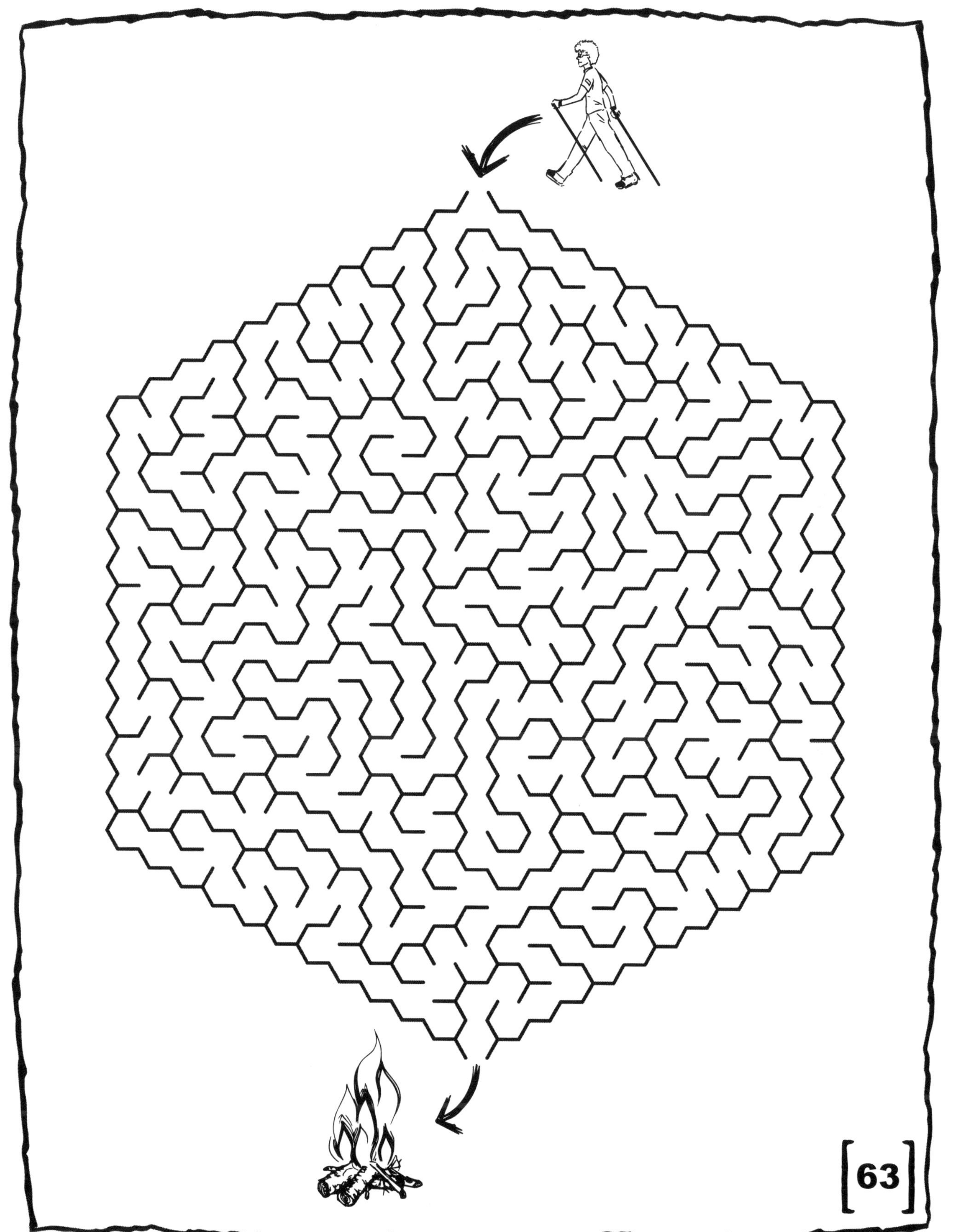

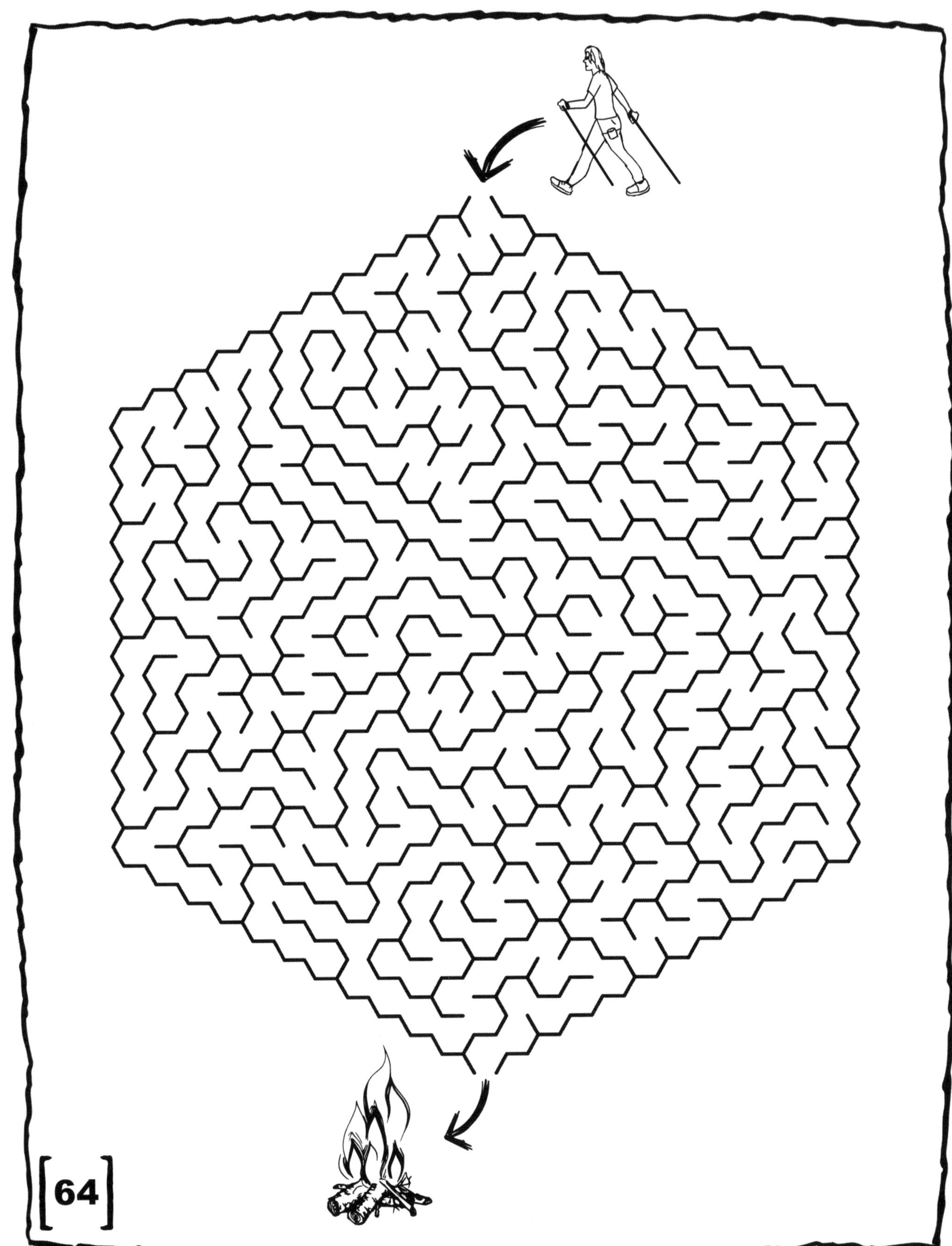

64

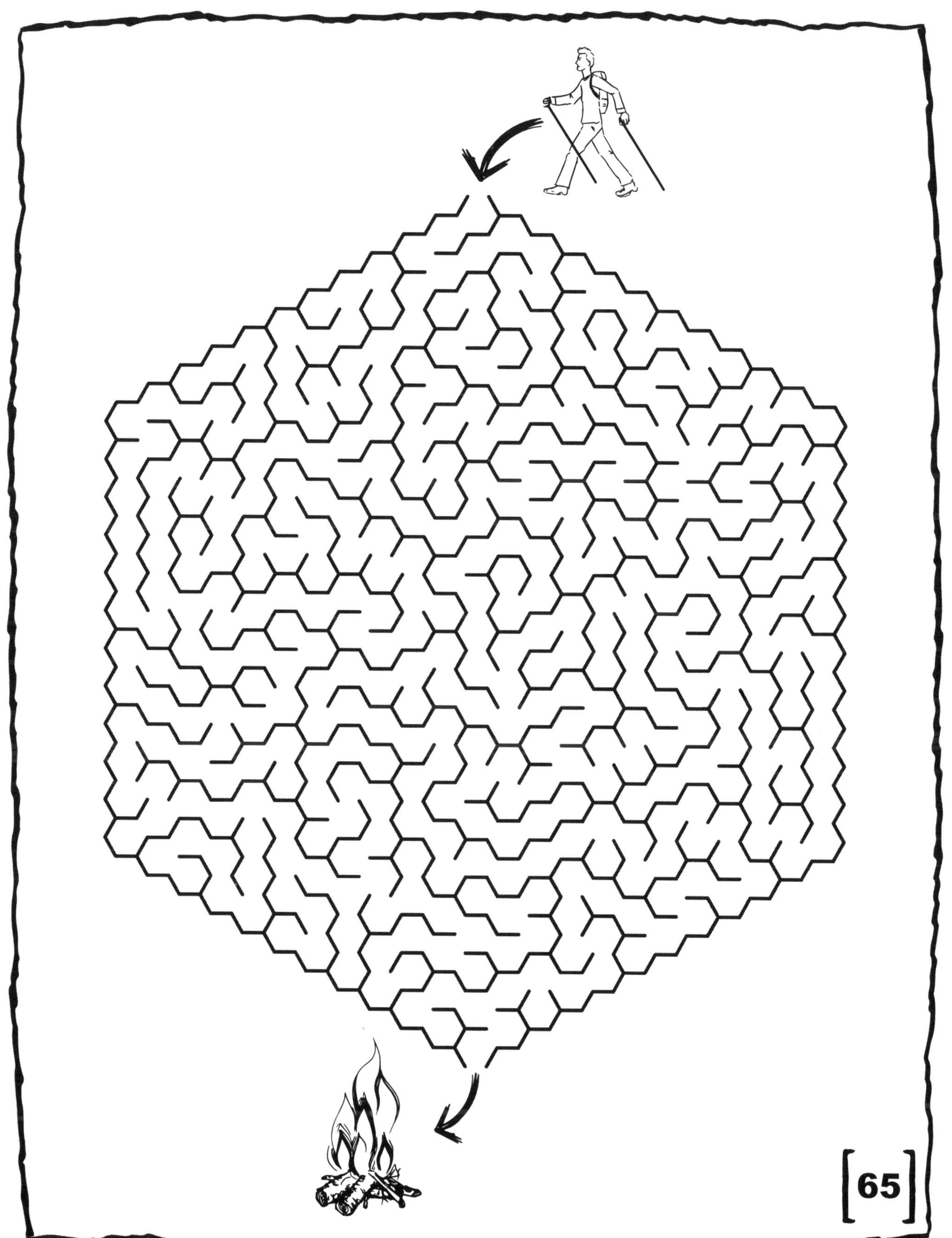

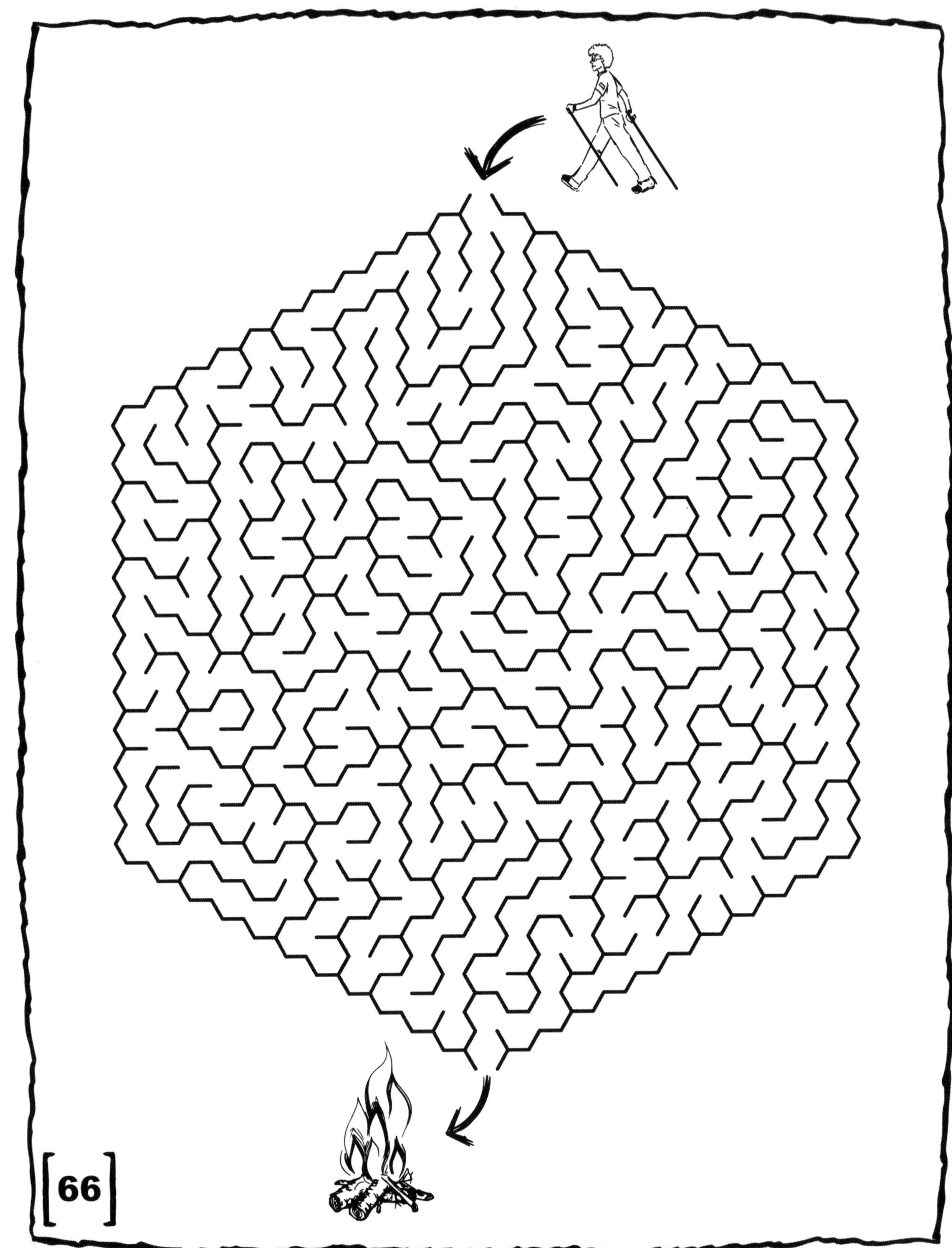

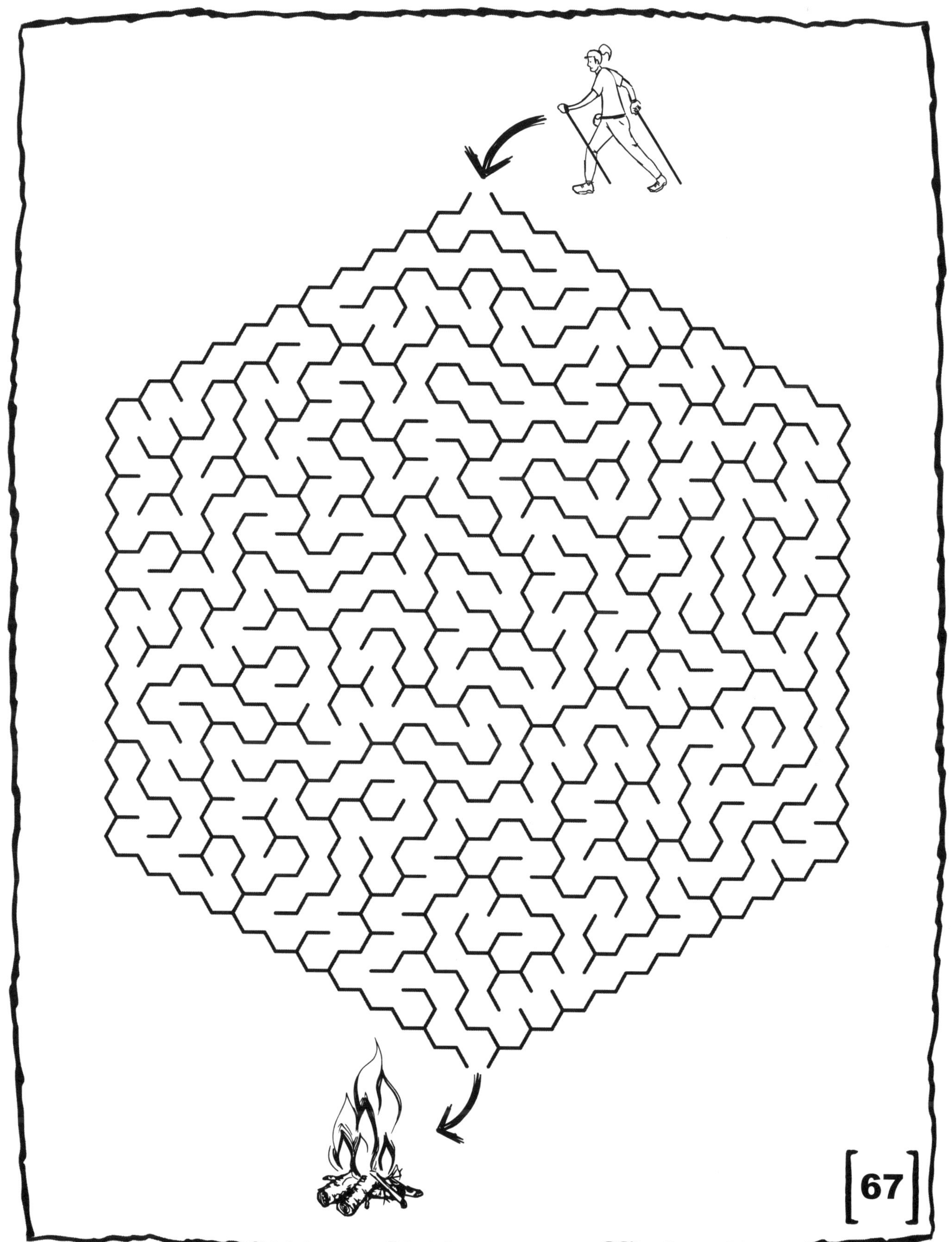

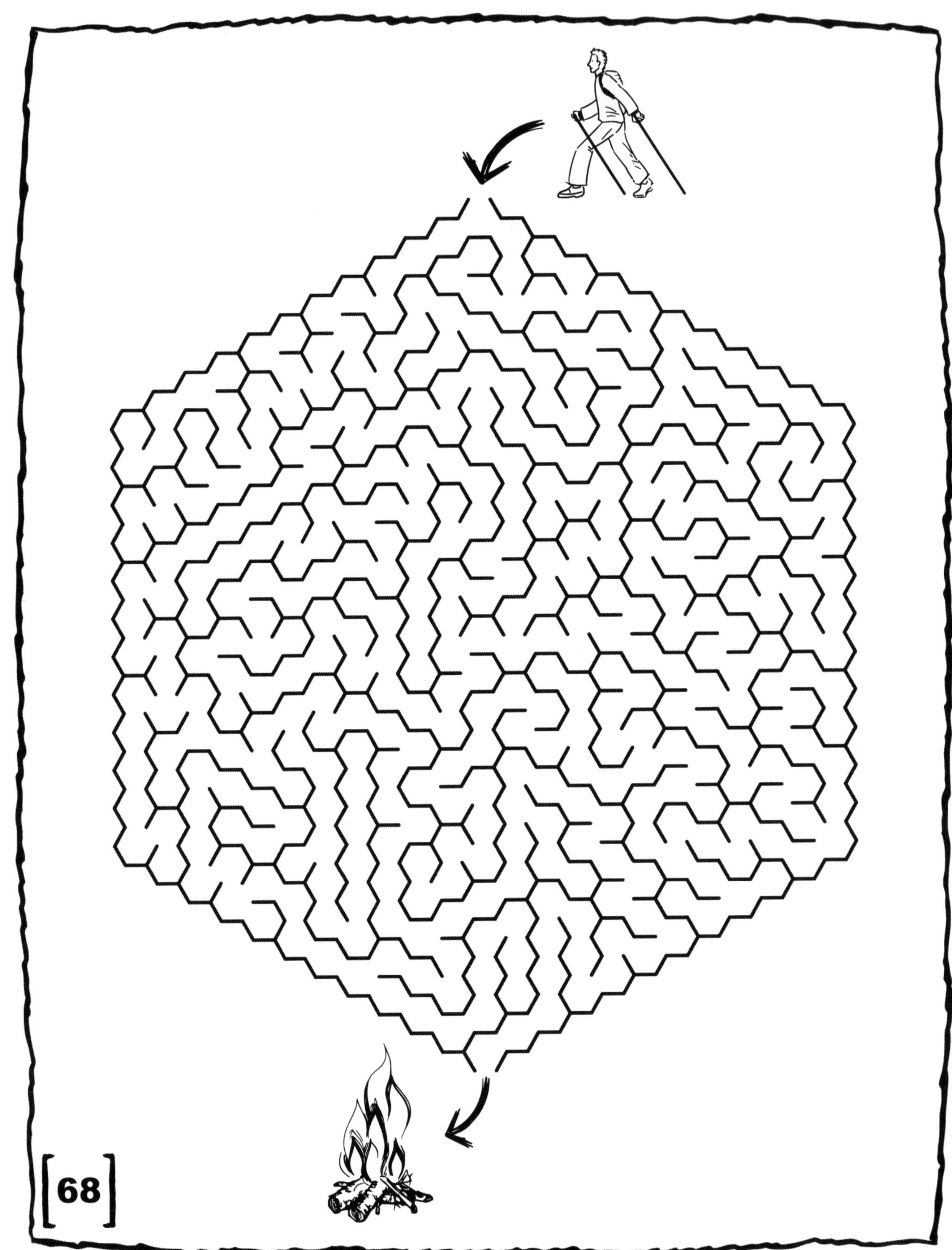

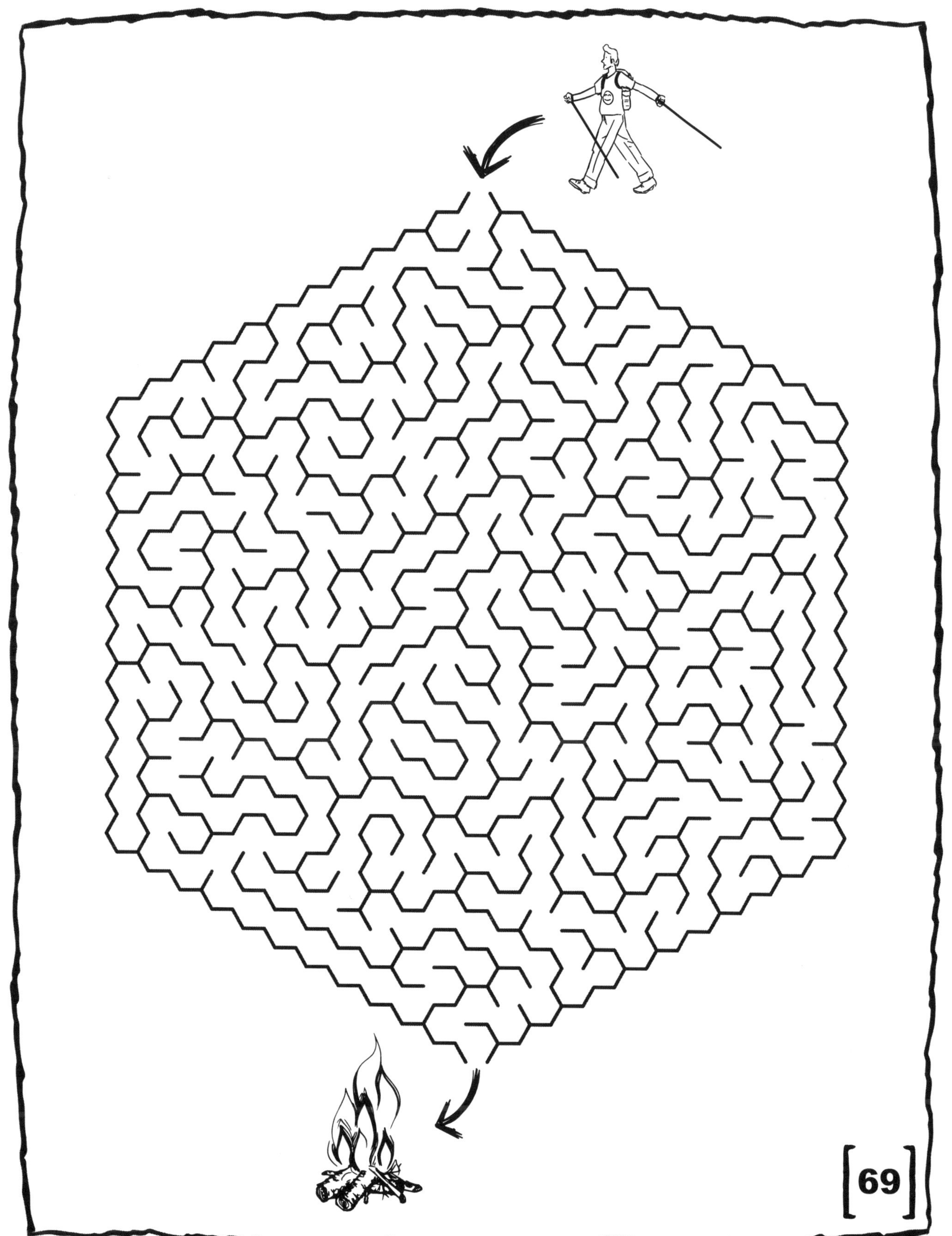

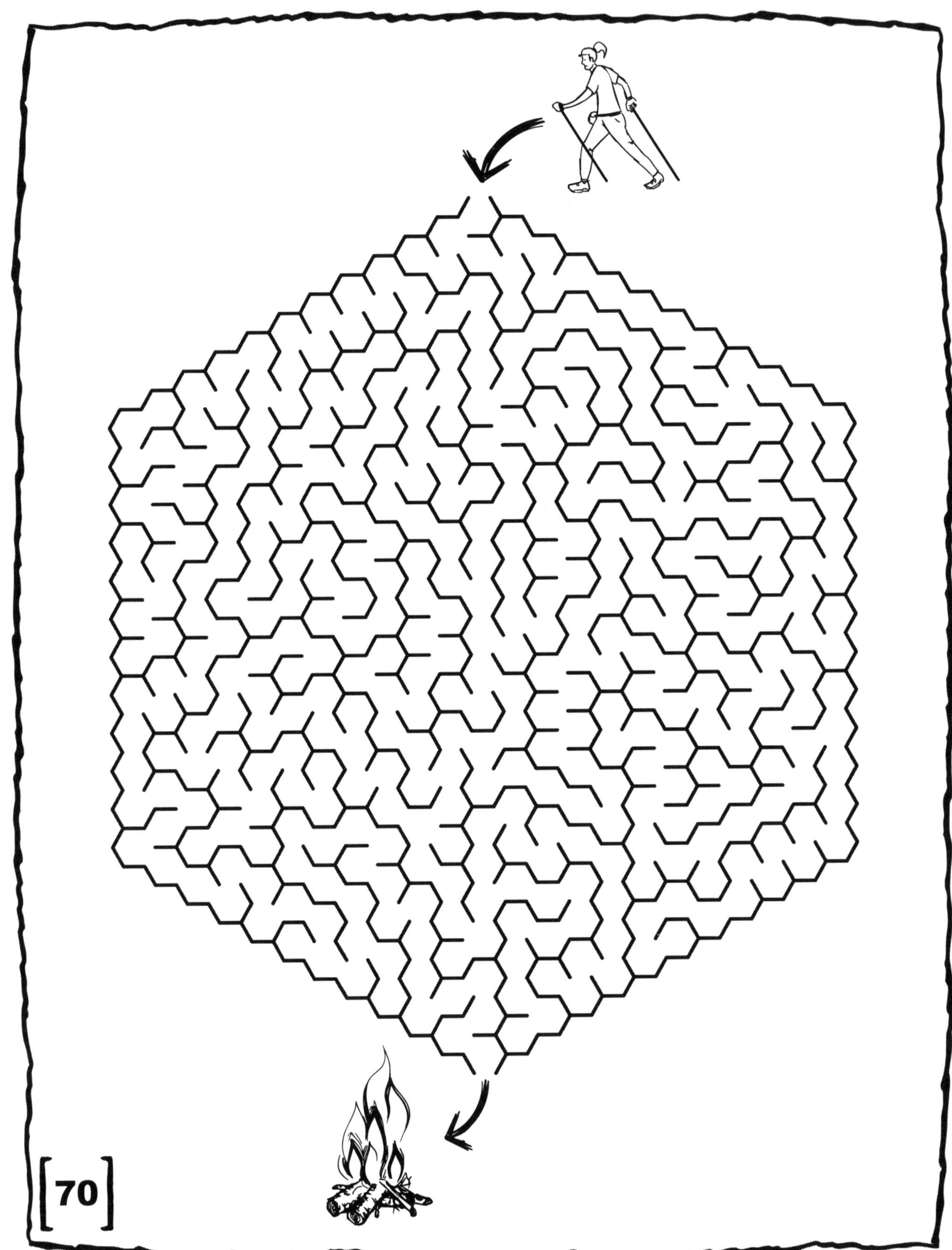

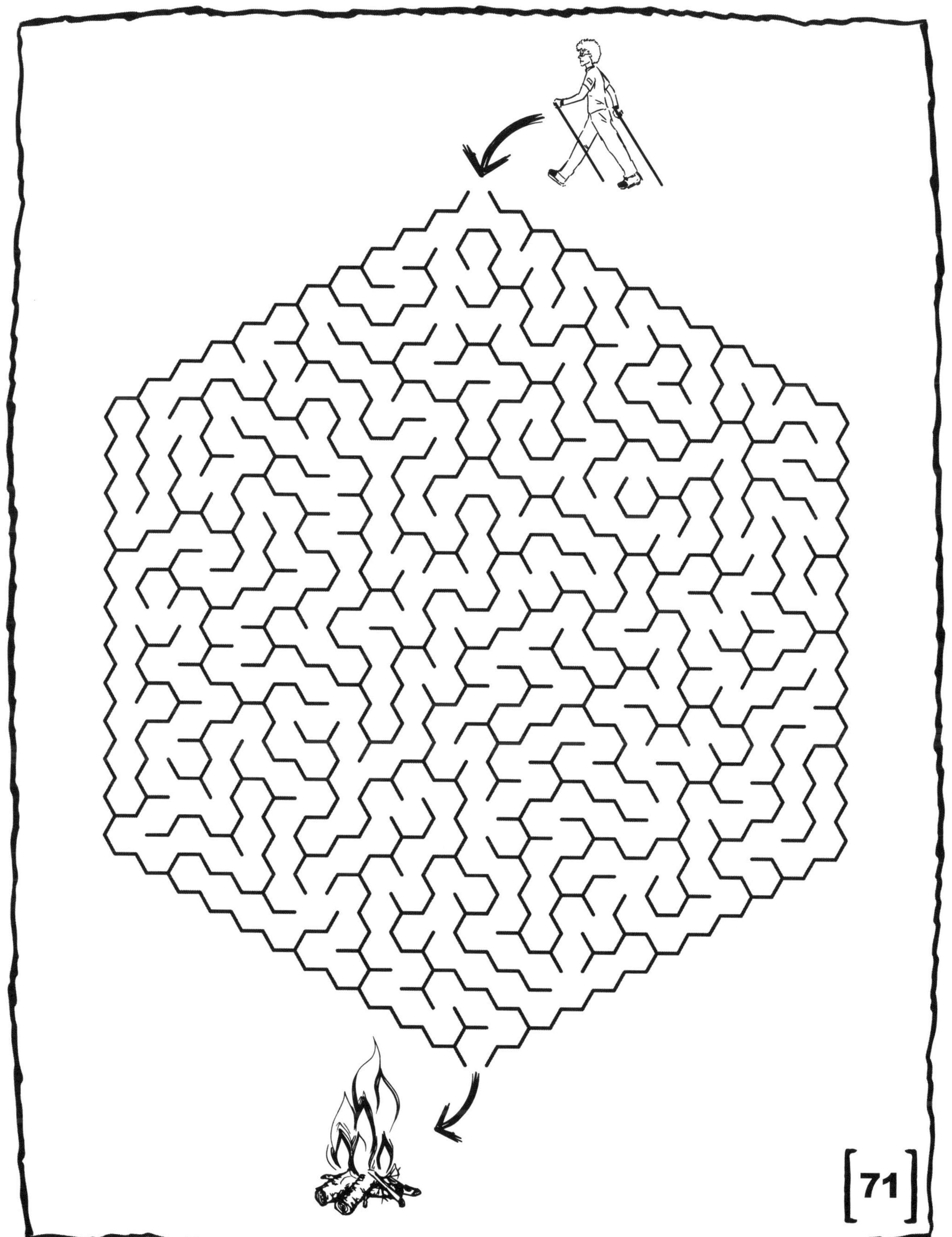

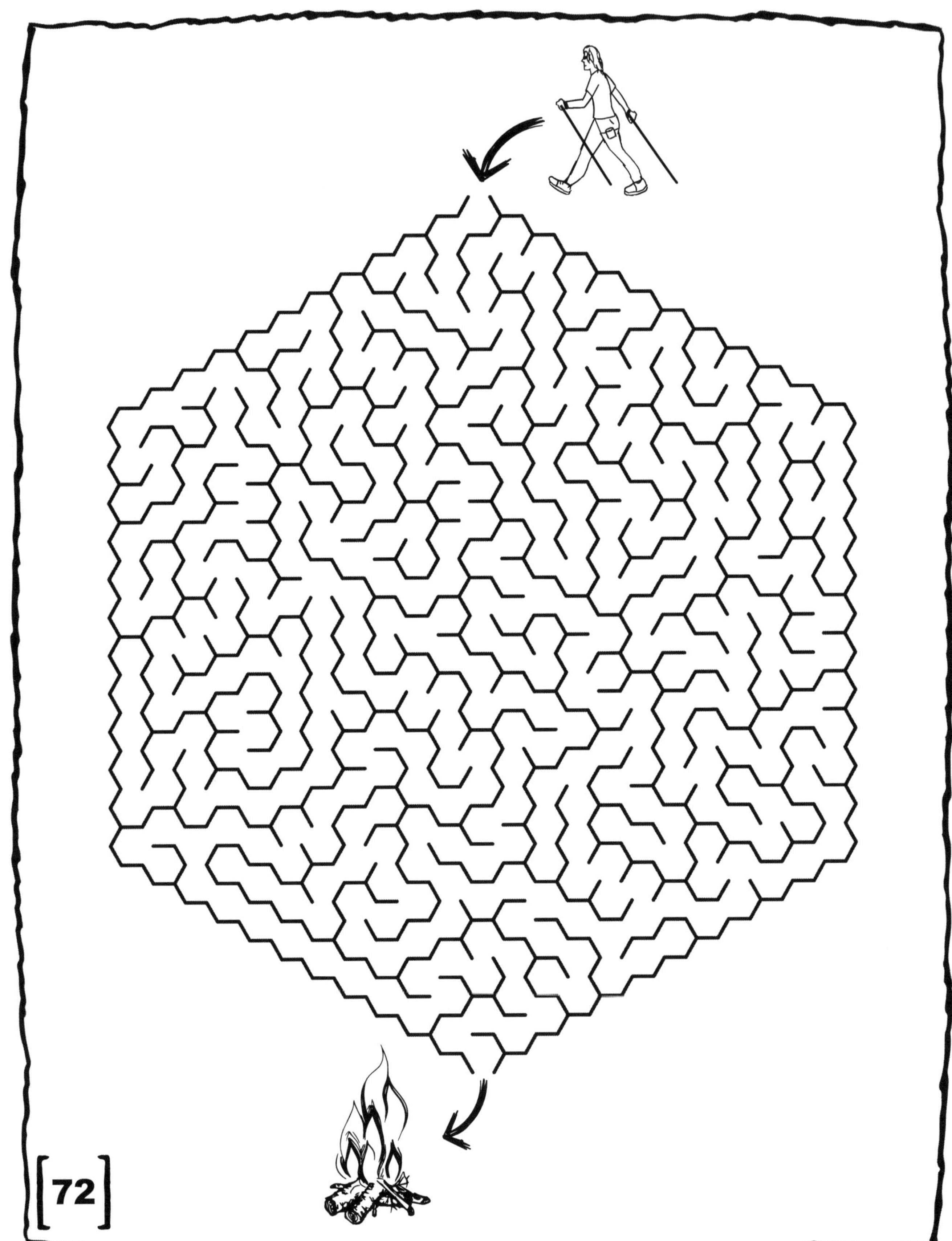

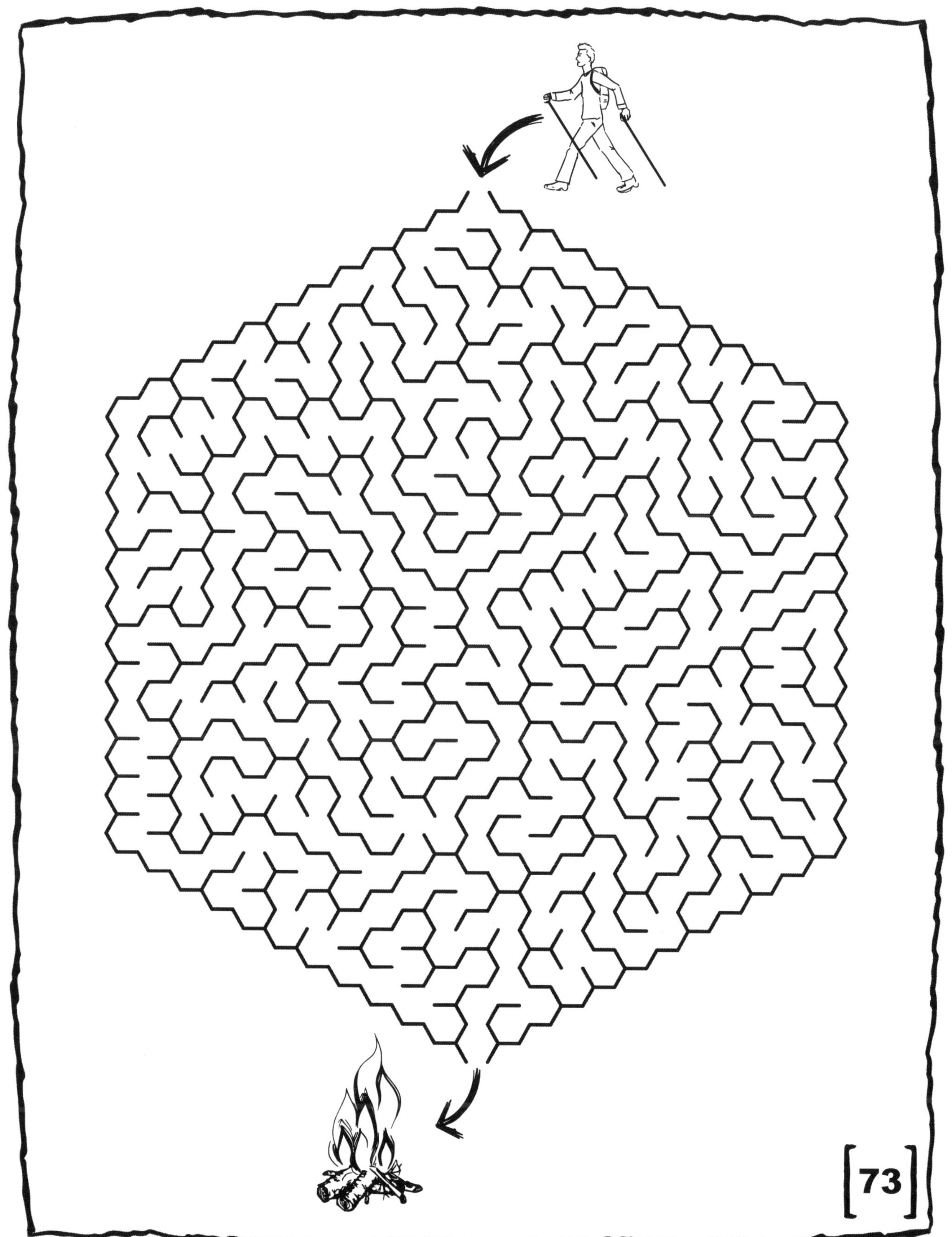

[73]

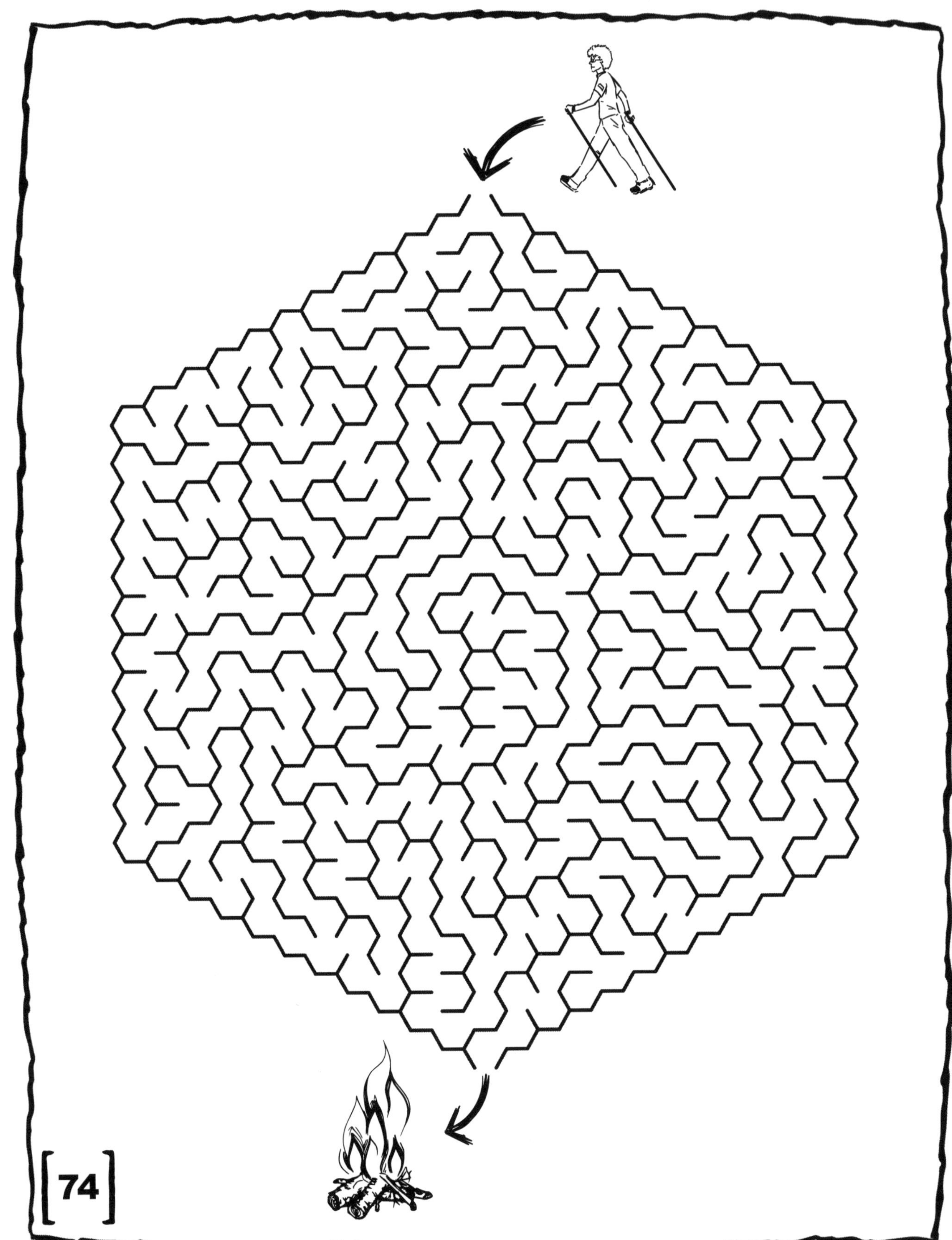

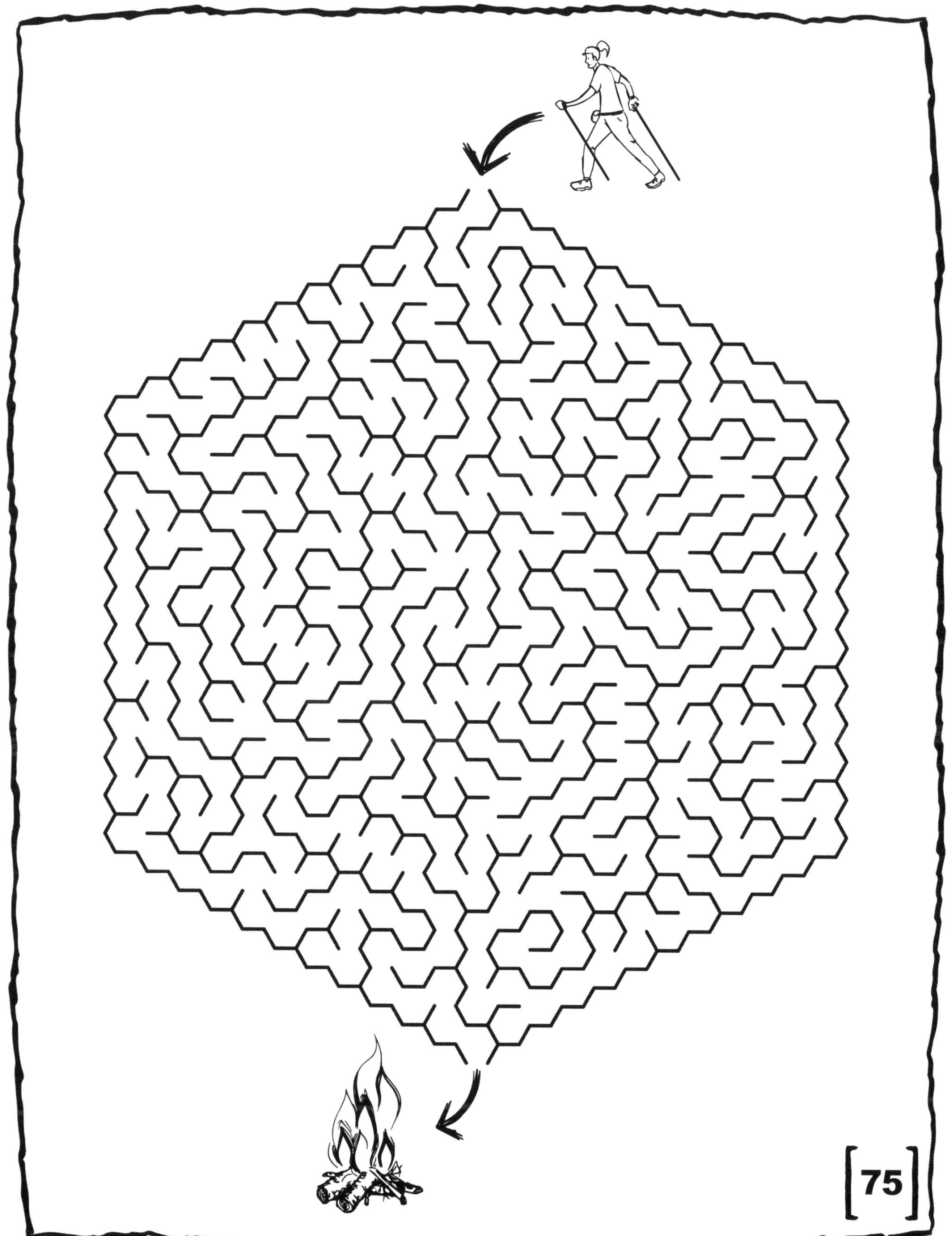

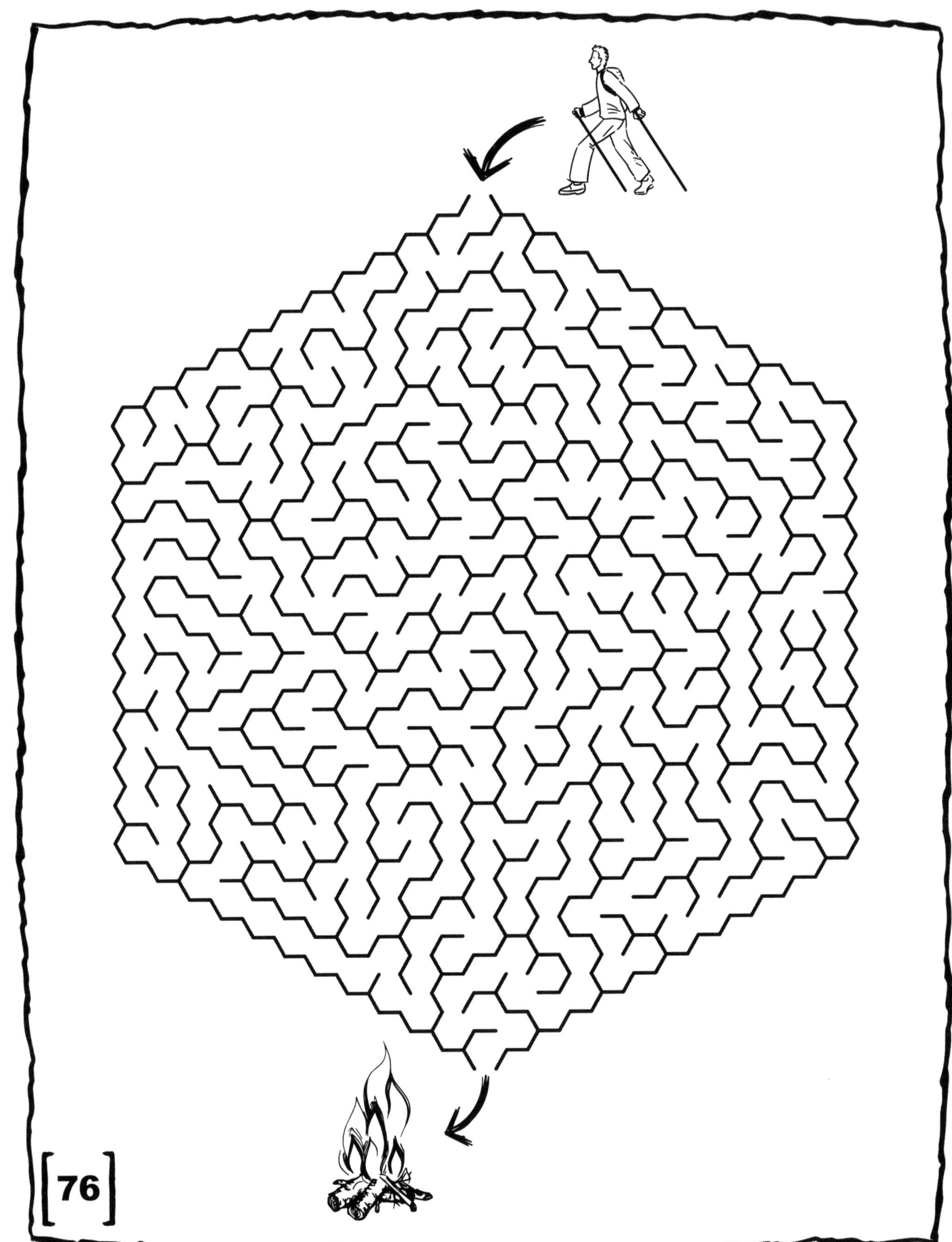

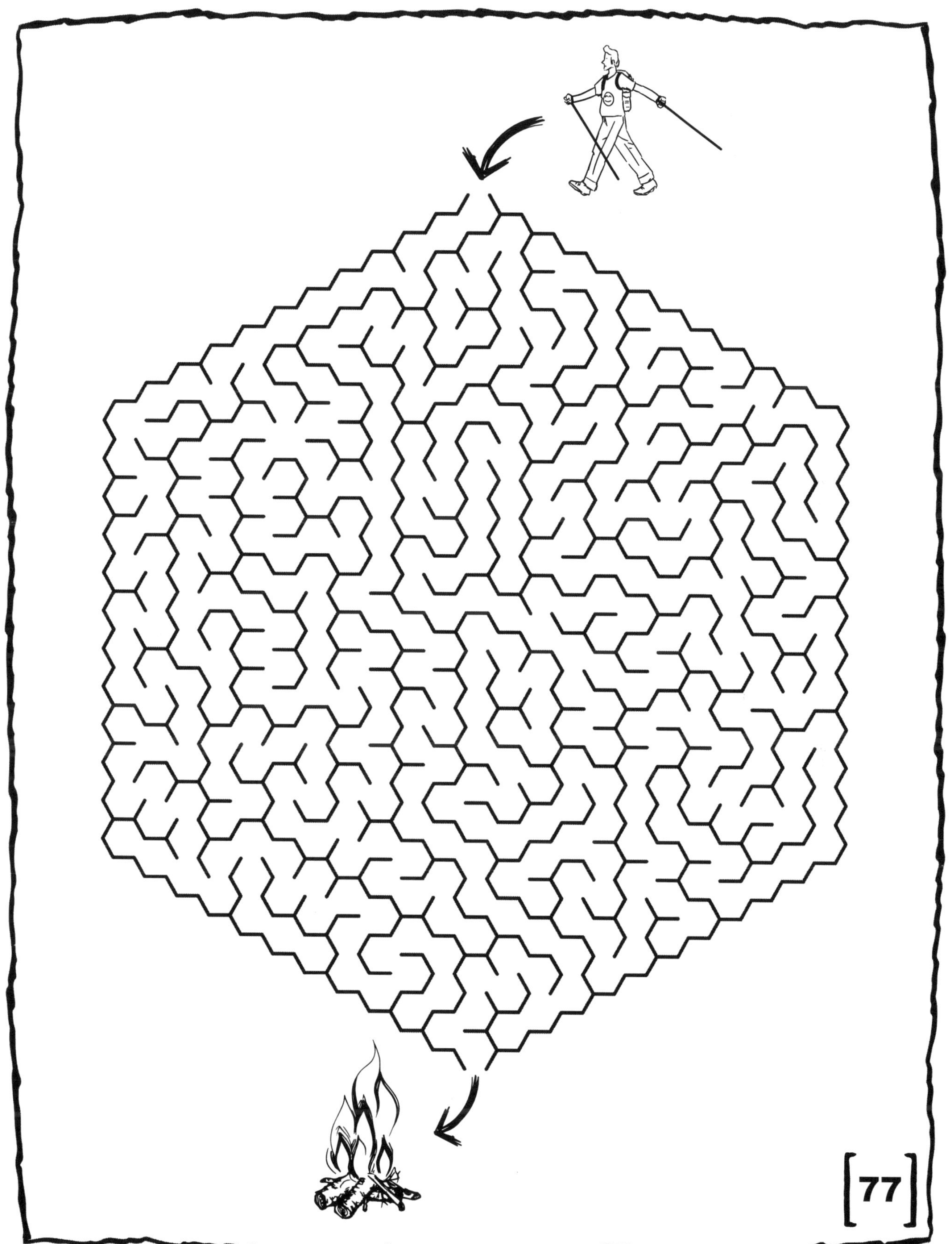

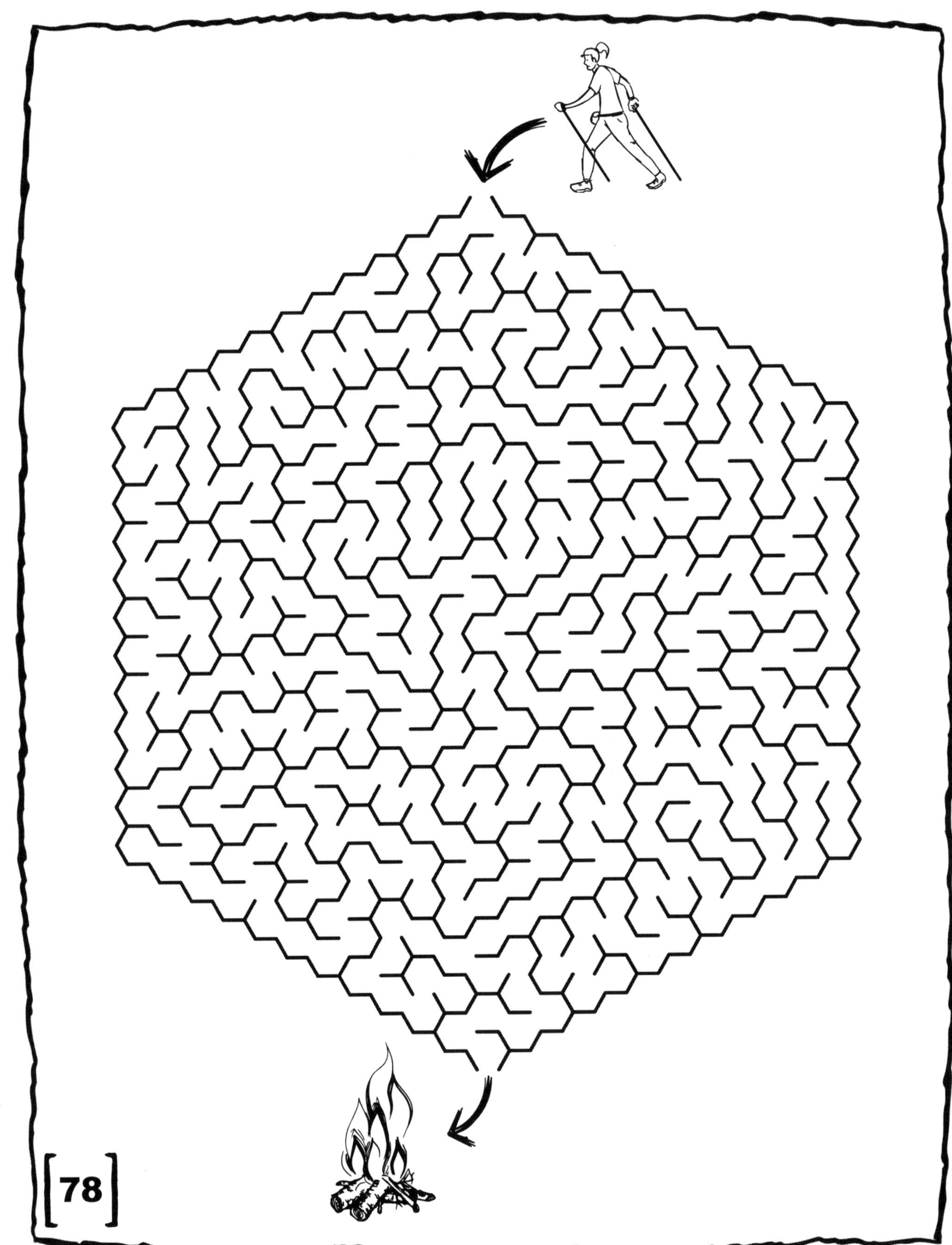

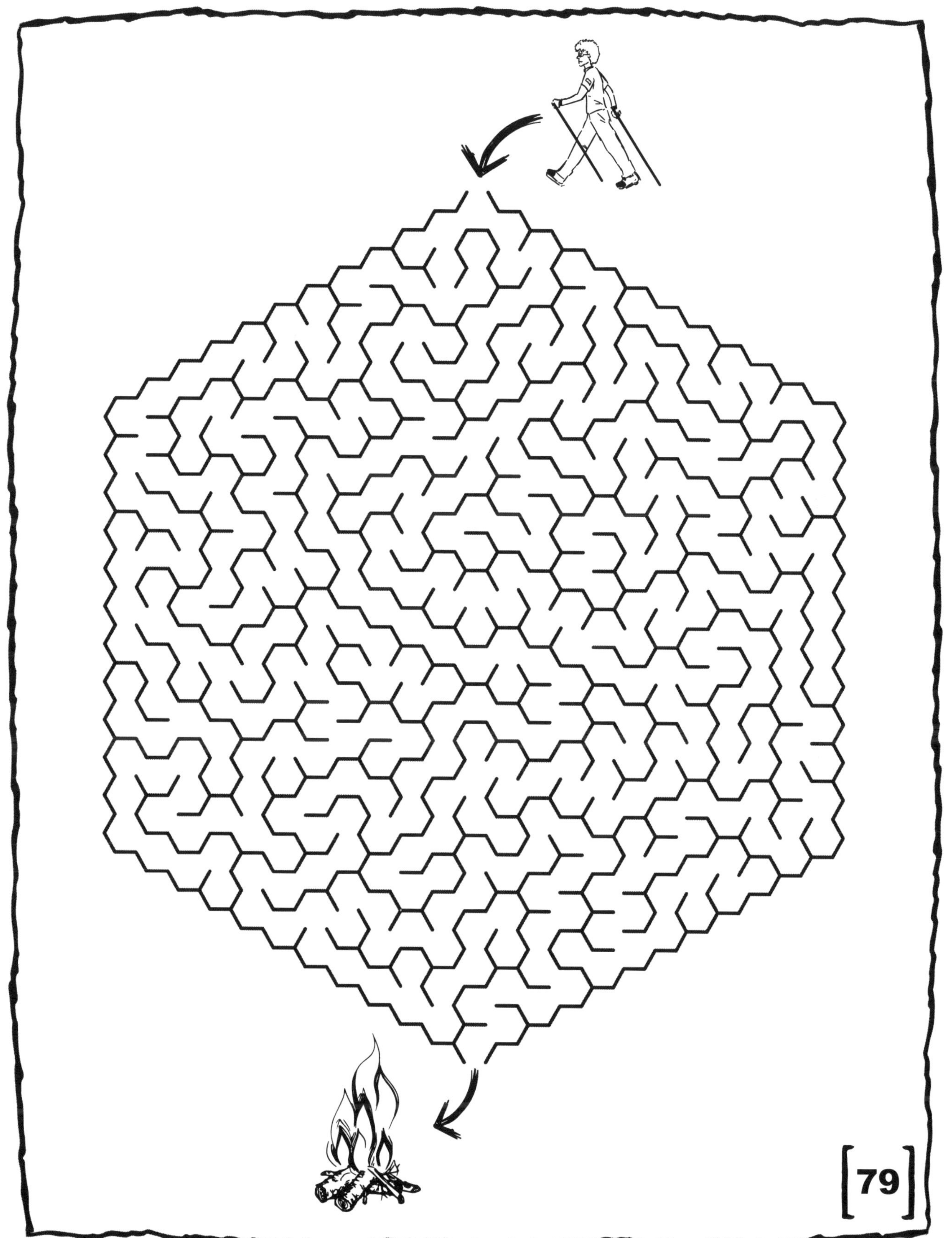

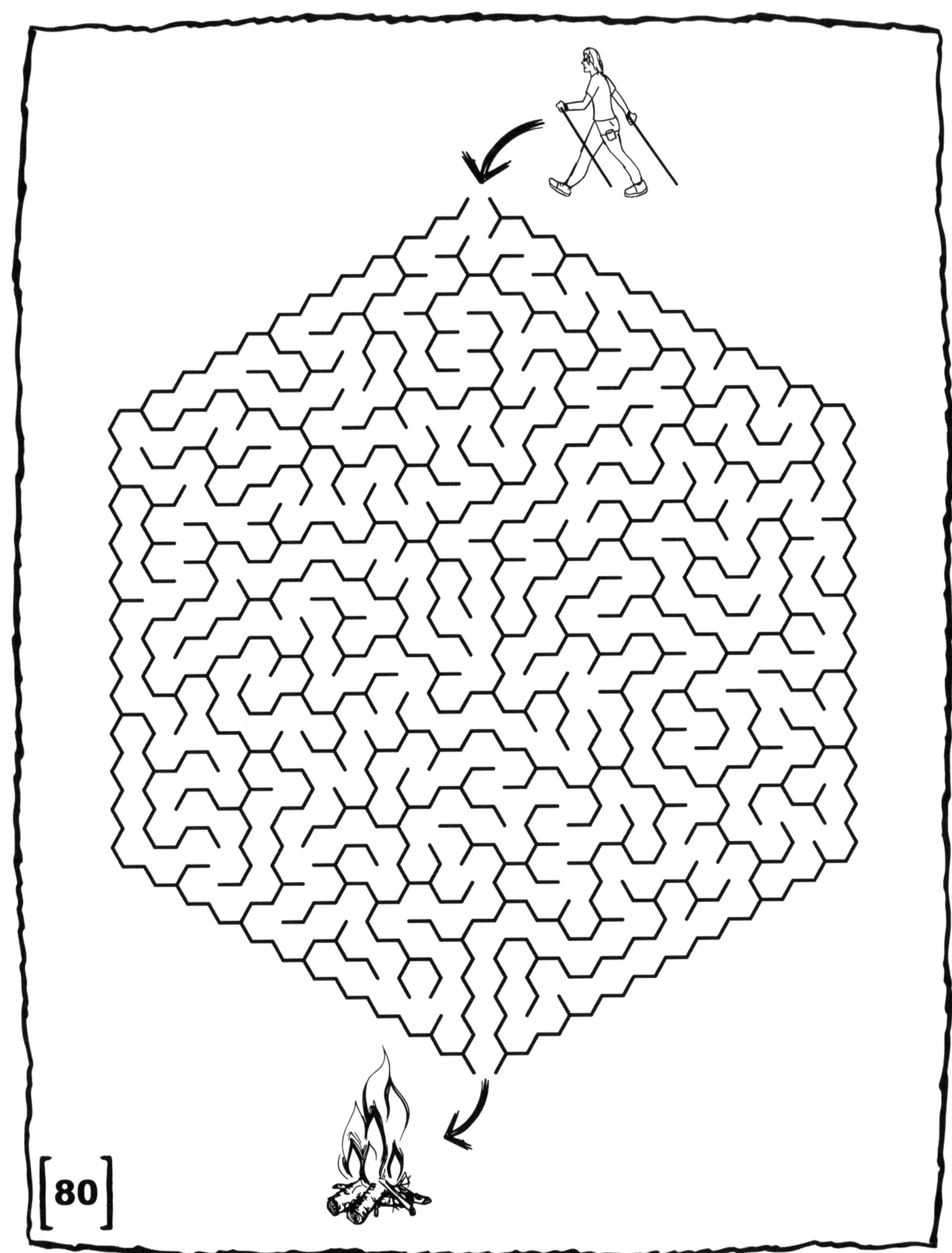

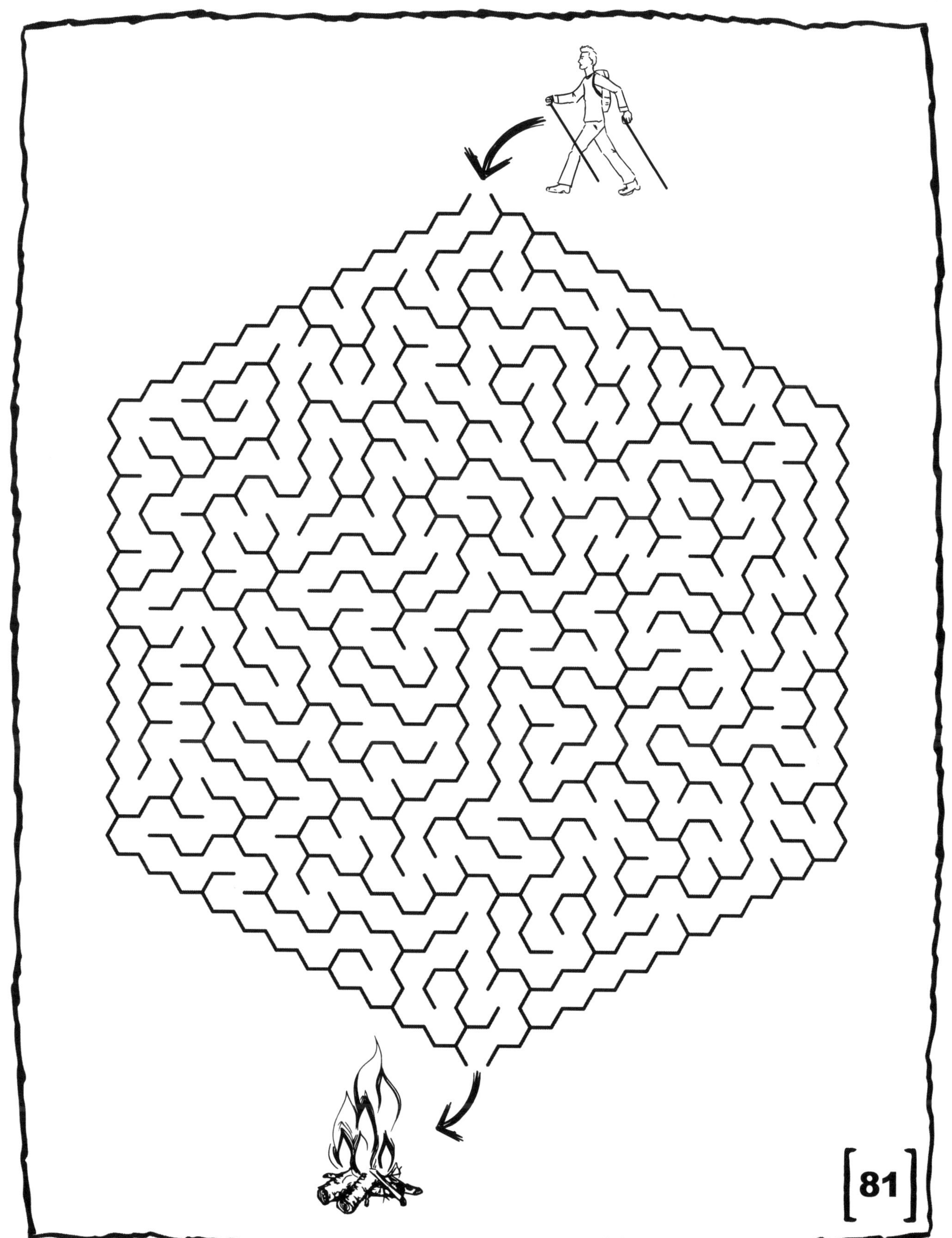

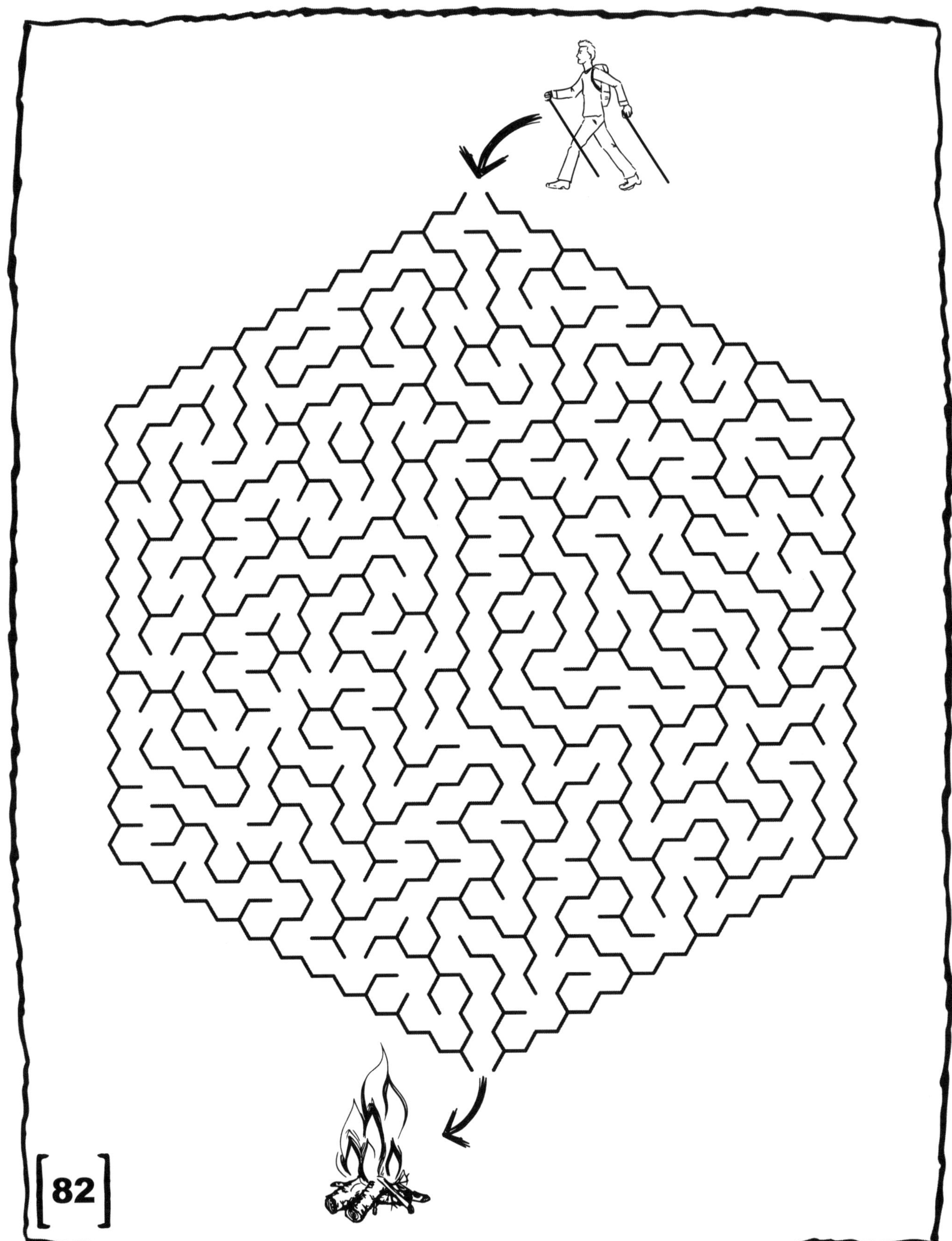

1

2

3

4

5
6
7
8

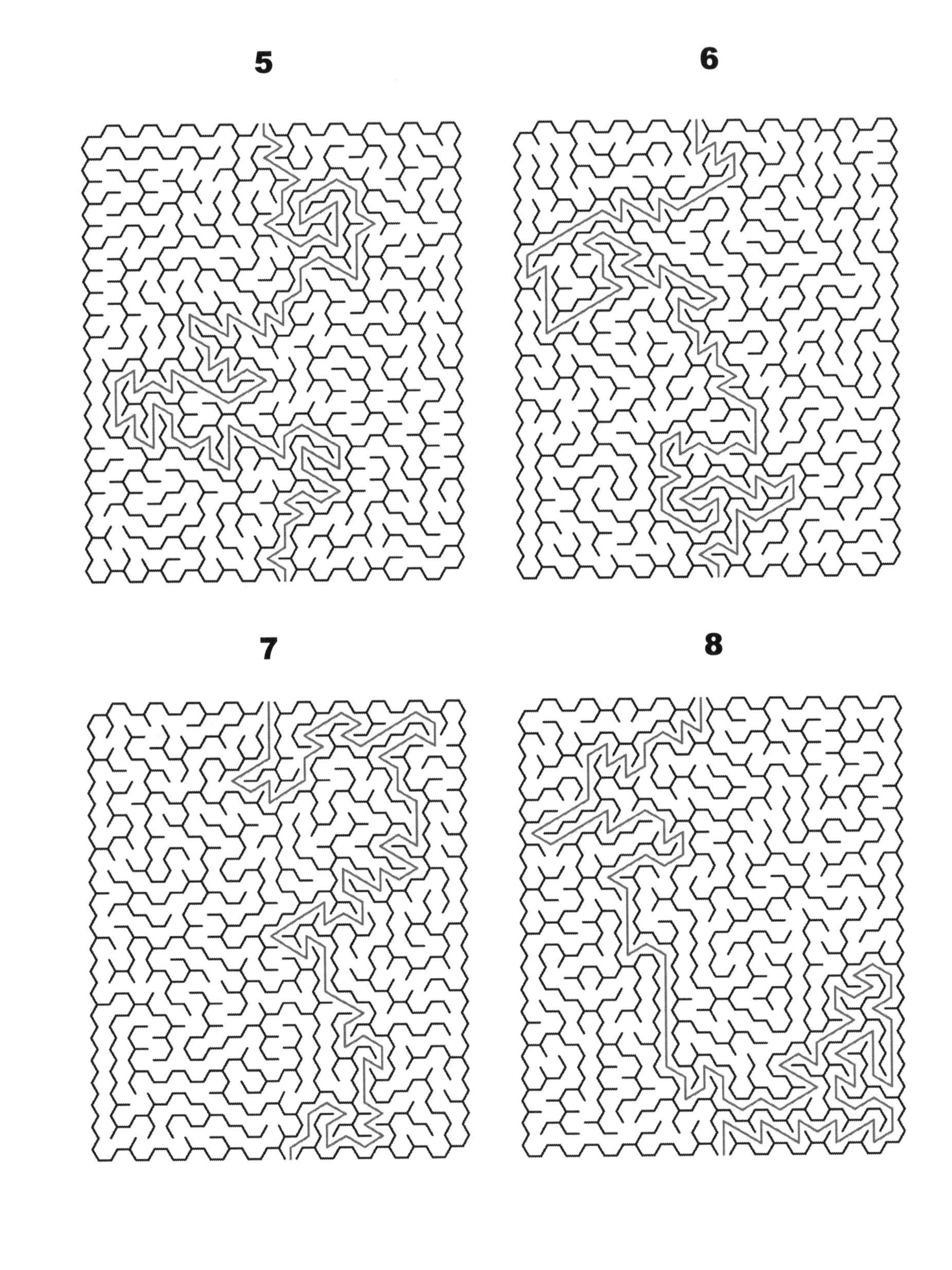

9

10

11

12

13

14

15

16

17

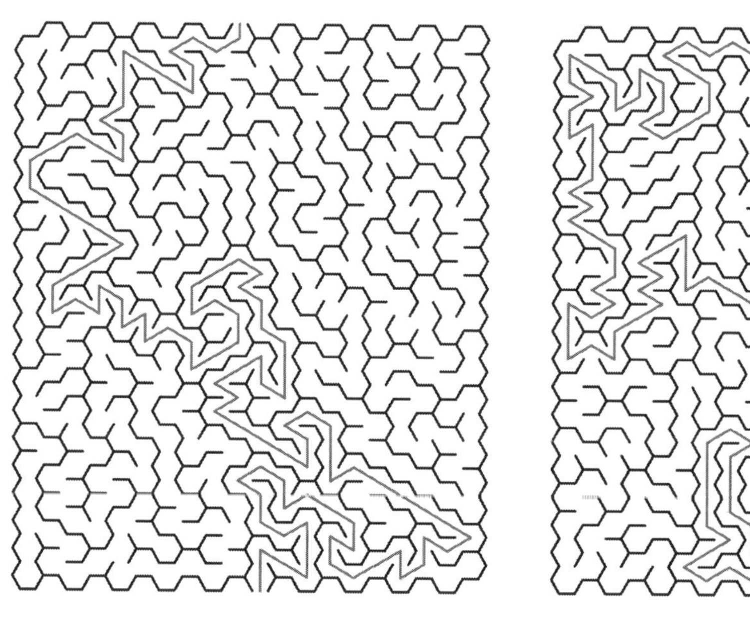

18

19

20

21

22

23

24

25

26

27

28

29

30

31

32

33

34

35

36

37

38

39

40

41

42

43

44

45

46

47

48

49

50

51

52

53

54

55

56

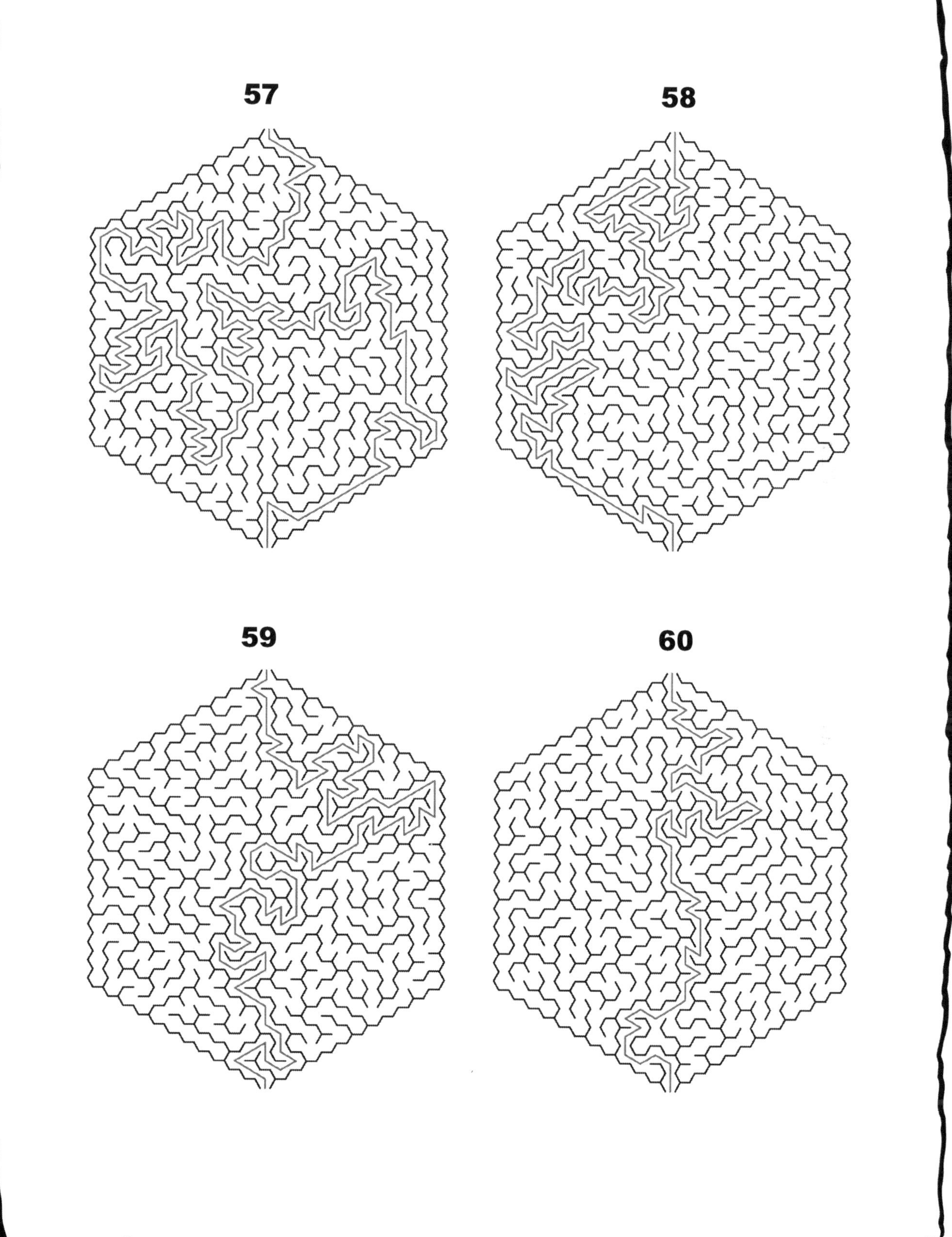
57
58
59
60

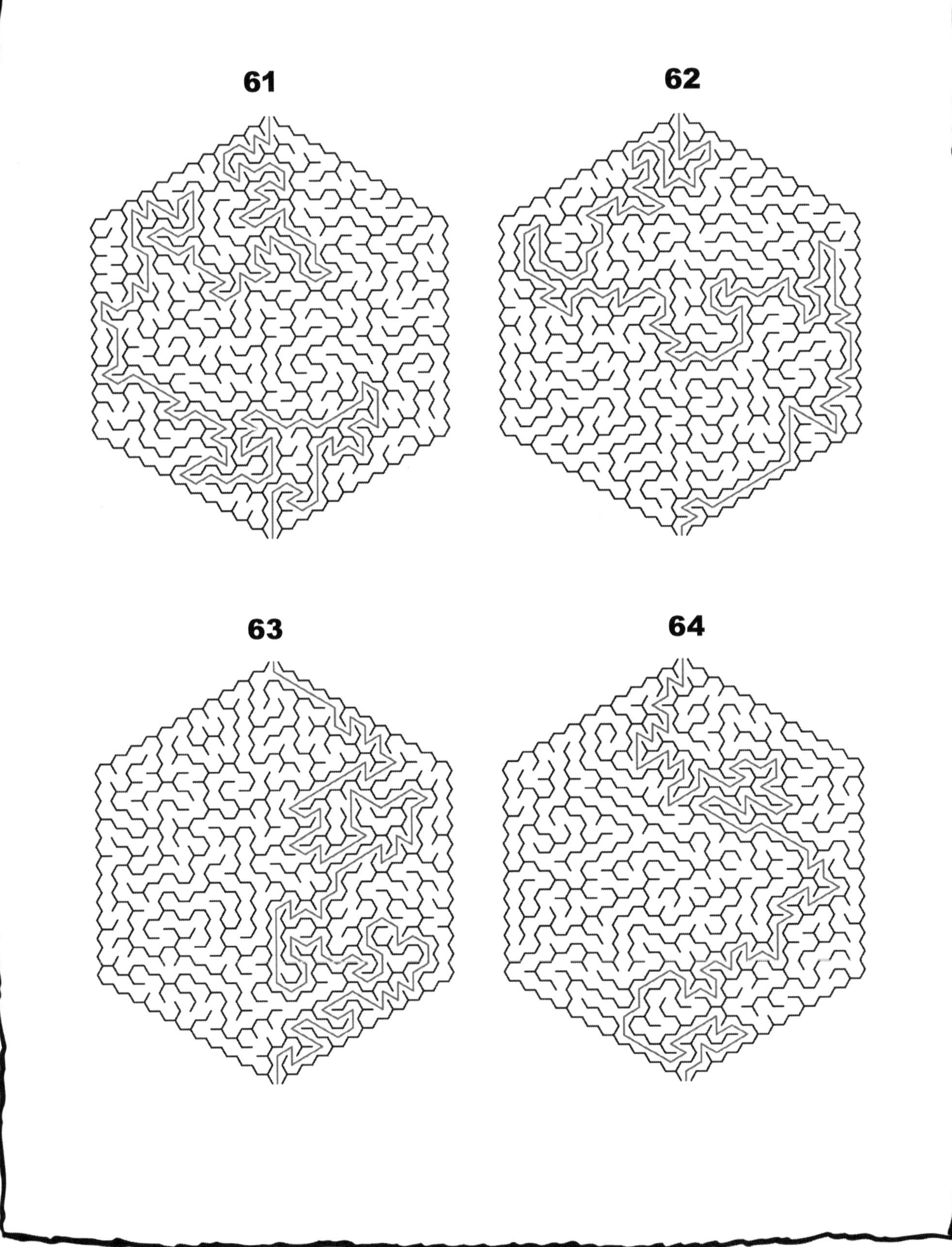

61
62
63
64

65

66

67

68

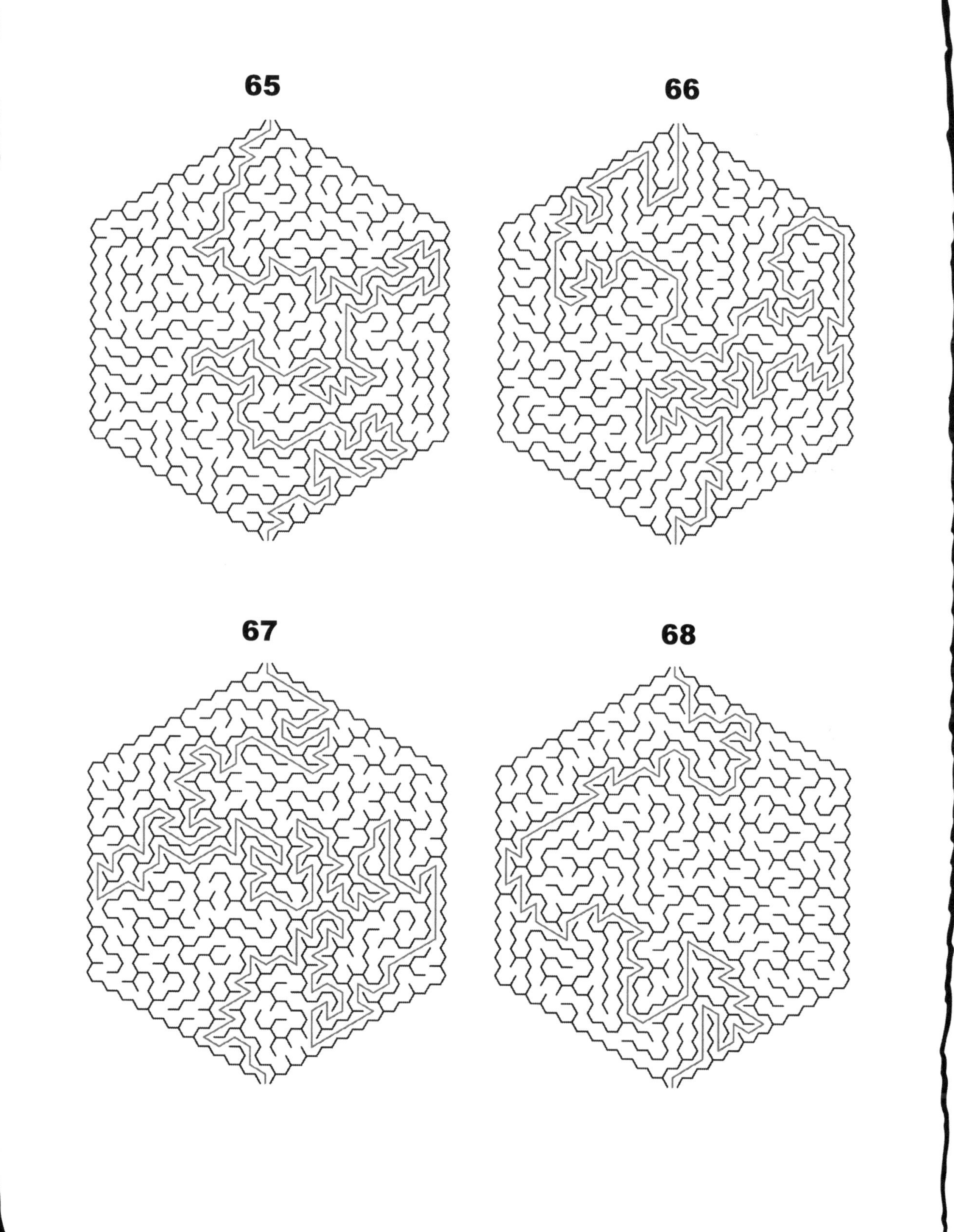

69

70

71

72

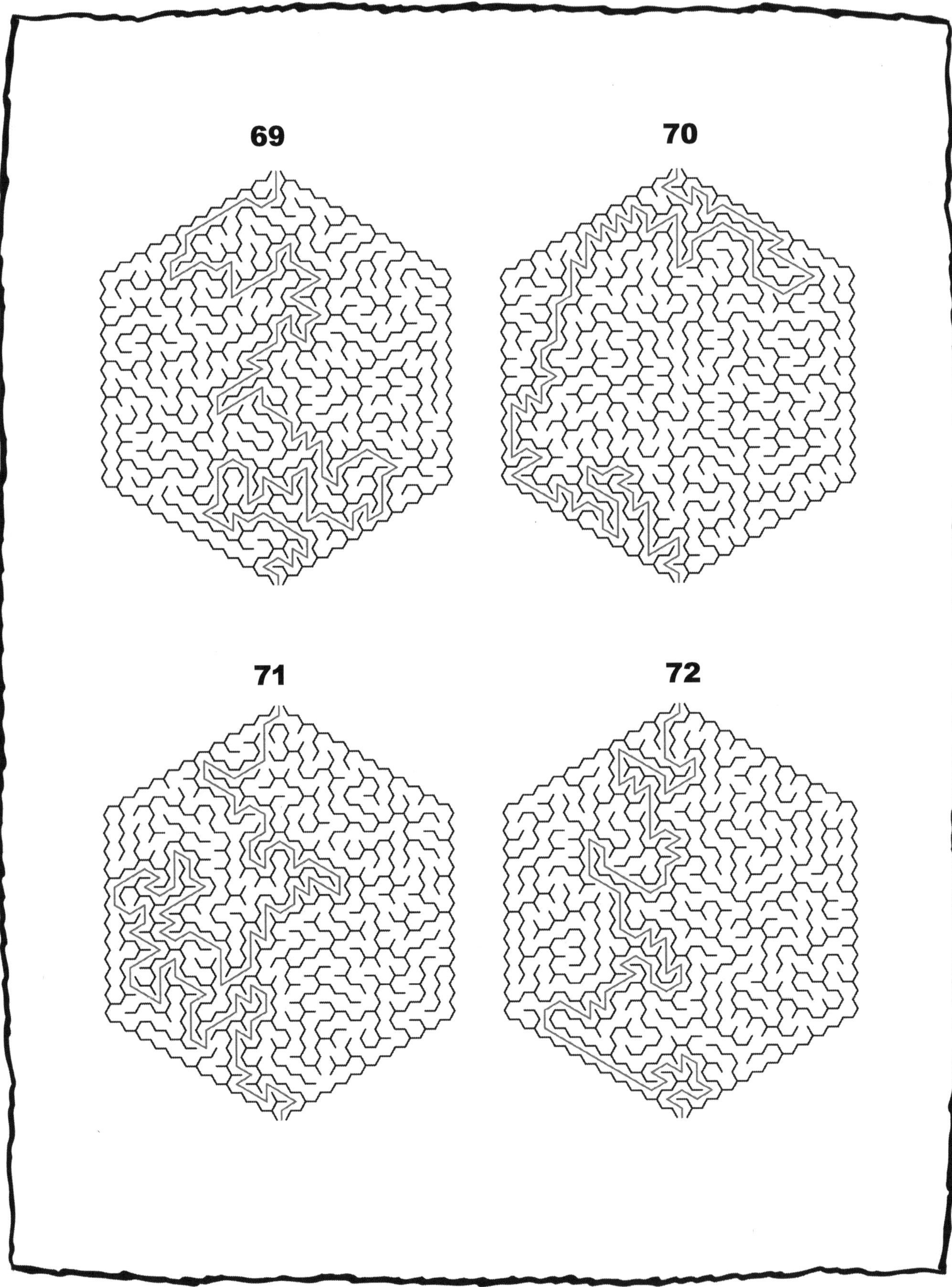

73

74

75

76

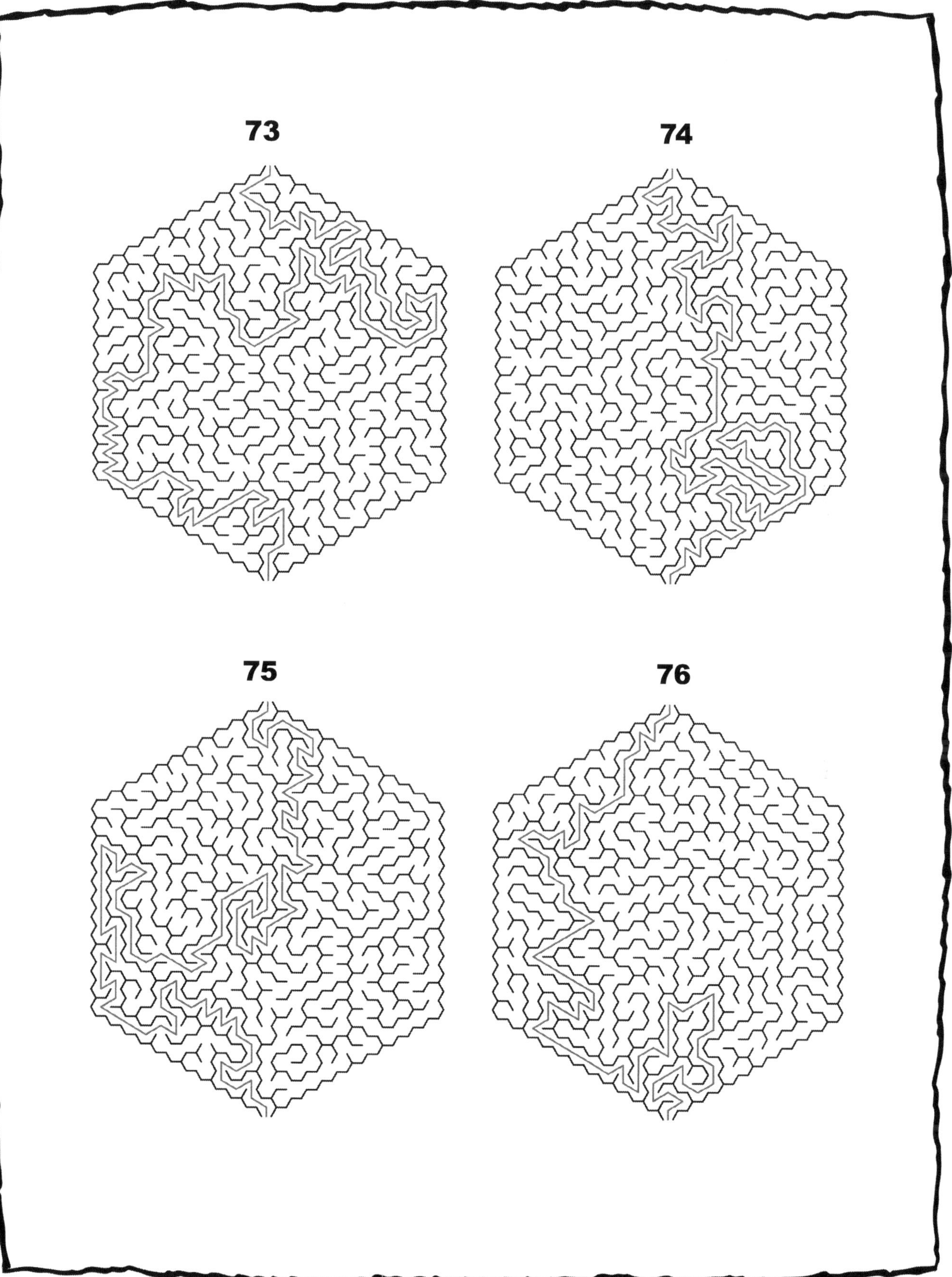

77

78

79

80

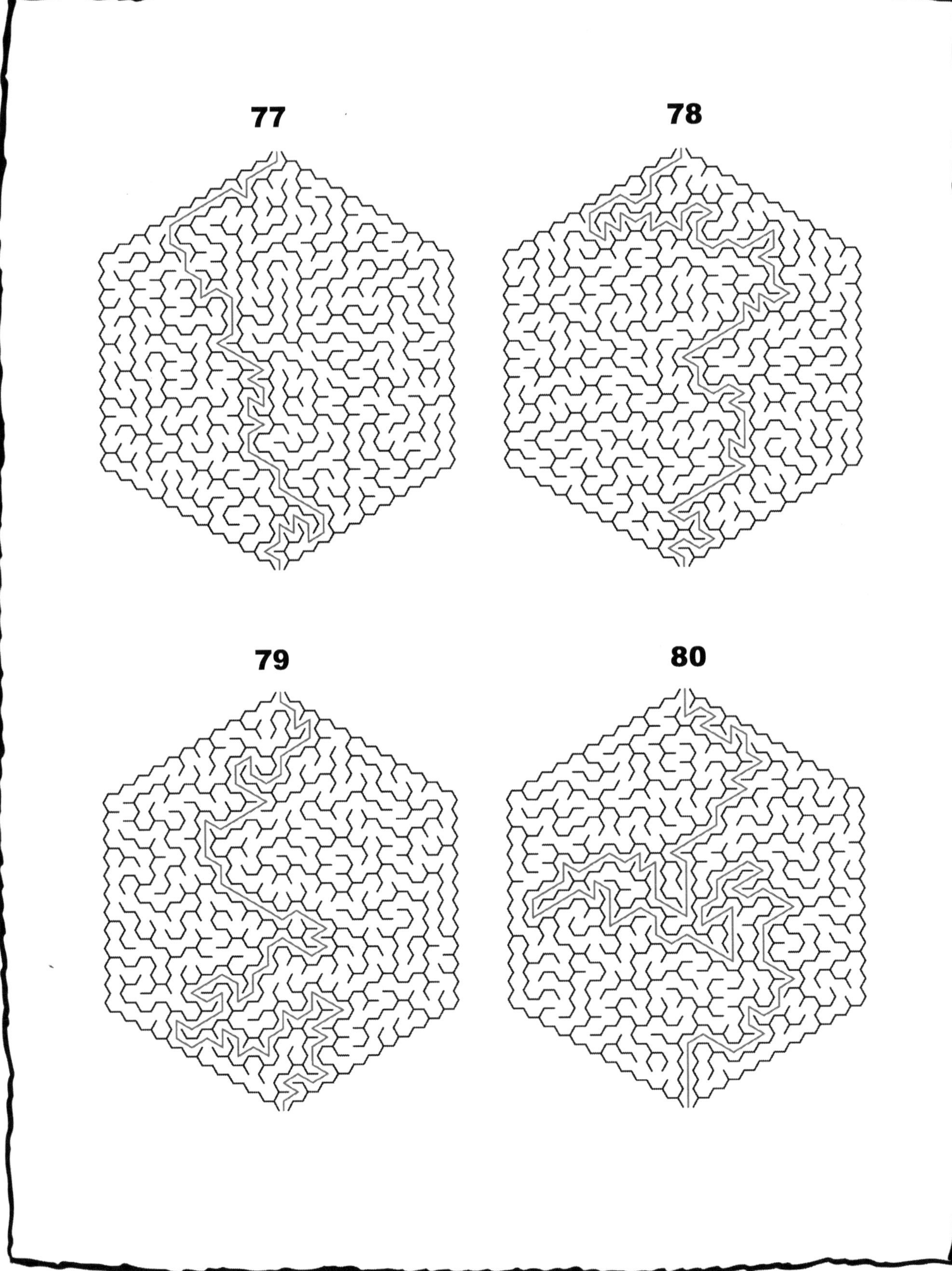

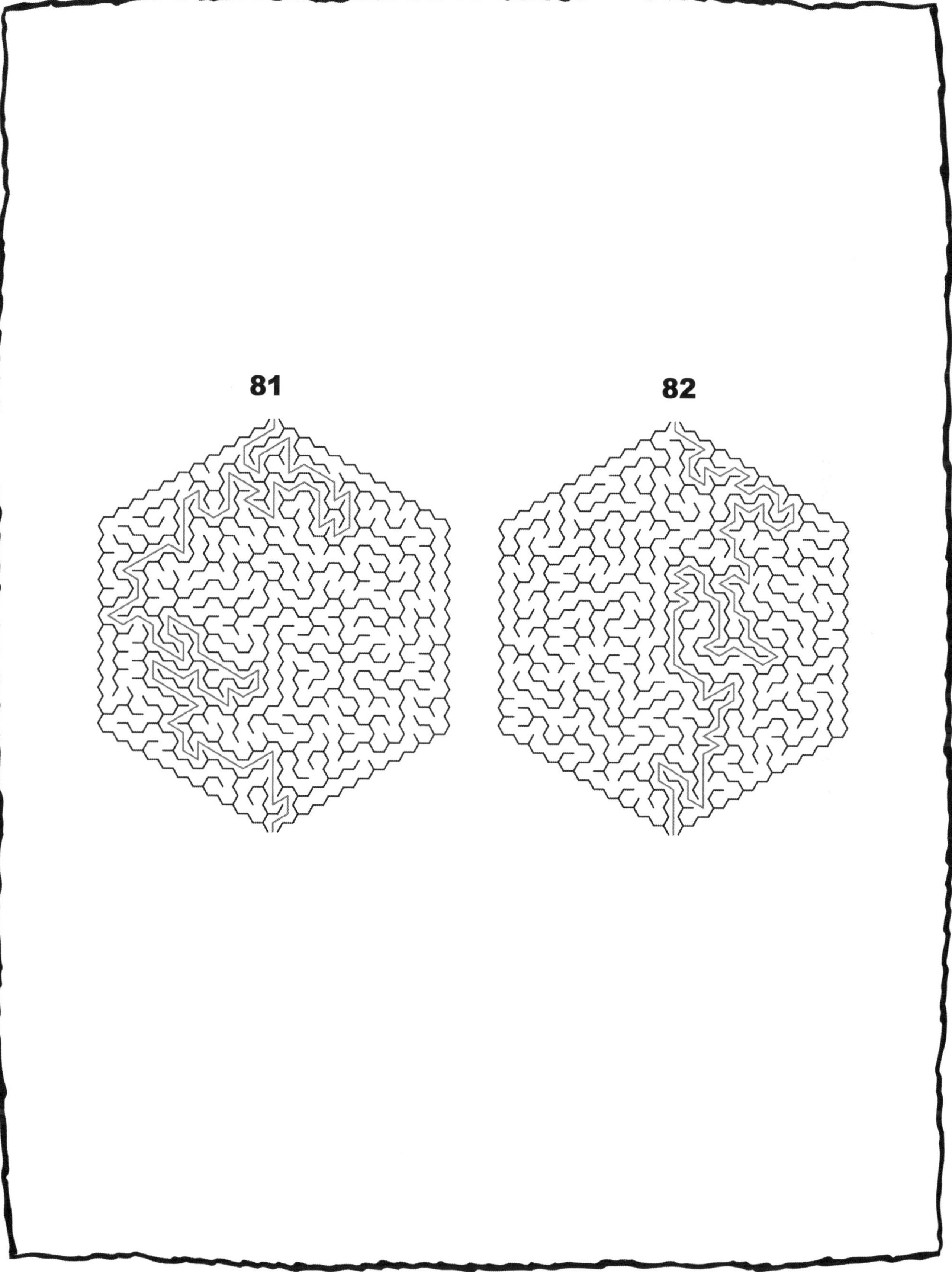

81
82

Made in the USA
Monee, IL
07 July 2026

56547090R00059